JOURNAL FOR THE STUDY OF THE OLD TESTAMENT
SUPPLEMENT SERIES

Editors
David J A Clines
Philip R Davies
David M Gunn

Department of Biblical Studies
The University of Sheffield
Sheffield S10 2TN
England

THE SENSE OF BIBLICAL NARRATIVE:

Three Structural Analyses in the Old Testament
(I Samuel 13-31, Numbers 11-12, I Kings 17-18)

David Jobling

St. Andrew's College,
Saskatoon, Canada

Journal for the Study of the Old Testament
Supplement Series, 7

Sheffield
1978

Chapters I and II have appeared, in somewhat
different form, under copyright of the Society
of Biblical Literature in its *Seminar Papers*.
The material is reused here by permission.

ISBN O 905774 12 4 (hardback)
ISBN O 905774 06 X (paperback)

ISSN 0309-0787

Published by
JSOT
Department of Biblical Studies
The University of Sheffield
Sheffield, S1O 2TN
England

1978

Printed in Great Britain by Fengraphic, Cambridge

Contents

Introduction   1

Chapter I
JONATHAN: A STRUCTURAL STUDY IN 1 SAMUEL   4

    0. Introduction   4
    1. The theological problematic of 1 Sam 13-31   5
    2. The character Jonathan in 1 Sam 13-31   6
    3. Approaches to the character Jonathan   14
    4. Conclusions   21

    Footnotes to Chapter I   23

Chapter II
A STRUCTURAL ANALYSIS OF NUMBERS 11-12   26

    0. Introduction   26
    1. Narrative analysis   28
    2. Semantic analysis   40
    3. The "myth" and its versions   56
    4. The extension of the analysis to other sections   58

    Footnotes to Chapter II   61

Chapter III
AHAB'S QUEST FOR RAIN: TEXT AND CONTEXT IN 1 KINGS 17-18   63

    0. Introduction   63
    1. The drought   67
    2. The combat on Mt. Carmel   71
    3. The two stories as one unit   77
    4. Appendices   81

    Footnotes to Chapter III   86

Postscript   89

    1. Retrospect   89
    2. Prospect   90

    Footnote to Postscript   92

Works Consulted   93

Indexes   99

Introduction

> Il est extrêmement difficile de parler du sens et
> d'en dire quelque chose du sensé ("It is extreme-
> ly difficult to talk of meaning and say anything
> meaningful about it"; Greimas, 1970: 7).

1.   The three pieces included in this volume are in many
ways different. They consider quite separate sections of Old
Testament narrative. They were prepared for different scholar-
ly audiences; respectively a working-group on narrative analysis (not necessarily structuralist), a working-group on structural exegesis, and an occasional seminar on the Hebrew Bible
as a whole. Only the third has been substantially rewritten
for inclusion with the other two; all three retain many of the
characteristics of occasional papers. Yet they share an out-
look, and broadly a methodology, and may appropriately be presented together. They appear in the order in which they were
written.

2.   It is usual for a book on structural exegesis to contain a substantial theoretical introduction. Such introductions
tend to cover the same ground, and I do not offer yet another
one here. Each analysis sufficiently explains, I hope, the
theory that it employs. The larger theoretical system behind
these analyses (with the exception of I.3.3, which employs a
broader literary method) is found in Propp, Lévi-Strauss (especially 1963: 206-31), and Greimas (especially 1966: 172-213;
1970: 157-83; 1971a), and it has been discussed in the context
of biblical exegesis by Patte and Calloud (1976b: 1-46). For
the reader who wishes to investigate these matters more deeply,
Patte (86-88) provides an excellent starting bibliography. But
none of these pieces was written as a demonstration of a method.
I thought of each, first of all, as a piece of practical exegesis. Methodology seeks generality, but method must remain ad
hoc. The object of analysis dictates the tactics for analysis,
within one's larger interpretive strategy. Thus it is that,
out of one methodological matrix, three such different analyses

have been born. I have tried to allow each of the biblical
sections to dictate the aspects of structuralist theory
appropriate to it.

3.   A postscript has, however, seemed to me as necessary
as an introduction was superfluous. Considering the three
studies for the first time together, I have become aware of
significant connections between them, and realized that they
raise methodological issues, and questions about the direction
of future work, which they do not answer. I have taken the
opportunity in the postscript (dropping the editorial "we"
which I have retained in the studies themselves) to offer some
thoughts on the broad issues which the studies have raised.

4.   The first analysis, "Jonathan", is easily accessible
to the non-specialist -- I venture to say this on the basis of
the responses of those who have read it. The second, frankly,
is less so. "Numbers 11 and 12" is a conscious attempt at a
"complete" analysis -- though, for reasons discussed in the
study itself, completeness cannot finally be achieved -- in
that it sets out to account for every detail in the text. It
is therefore extremely intricate. But Lévi-Strauss has taught
me, mostly by example (1969, 1973, and his other analyses of
myth), that if we do not account for the details, then we
account for nothing! The reader who survives it should find
in "Ahab's Quest" both relief and a challenge; relief, in that
I pursue a limited goal and consciously try to minimize technical terminology, and a challenge in that, leaving the analysis
incomplete, I indicate lines along which it could be continued
and deepened.

5.   The system of decimal paragraph numbers, replacing
cumbersome subheadings, is by now probably familiar. It is by
these numbers that the hierarchical organization of each chapter is indicated, and careful attention to them will greatly
facilitate the reading especially of Chapter II. A zero in
this decimal system always implies <u>introductory</u> comments, even
when this is not specifically stated. The numbers provide
also, of course, for cross-referencing within a chapter; in
the few instances where cross-references are <u>between</u> chapters,
I place the Roman chapter number before the decimal (e.g.,
II. 1.231). To minimize footnotes, the references to secondary literature are included in the text, and can be unambigu-
ously determined by reference to the list of "Works Consulted".

6.   My title is in deliberate imitation of A.-J. Greimas's
Du sens. The narrative of the Bible, like other human products,
"makes sense", that is, creates meaning. But what sense it
makes, the structuralists tell us, is a question inseparable
from how it makes any sense at all. So, to borrow a phrase
from Stephen Crites, these studies are explorations of "how the
Bible means".

        I wish to express my thanks to Daniel Patte, for his
unremitting work on behalf of structuralist exegesis, and
specifically for his invitation to me to prepare a paper ("Numbers 11 and 12") for his working-group at the Society of Biblical Literature; and to Karen Lanier, for the arduous typing of
the manuscript.

                                        New York
                                        March, 1978

Chapter I
Jonathan:
A Structural Study in 1 Samuel

> Only after the function and structure of the
> work itself have been studied should the more
> traditional tasks of relating it to history or
> psychology or of establishing its connections
> with other disciplines or with the world be
> undertaken (De George: xxii).

> Some psychologist has proved that Benjy is not
> a true psychotic but a literary construct. This
> being so, it is fortunate that Benjy is in a
> book, where he belongs (Scholes and Kellogg: 199).

0.   Introduction

0.1   That the narrative parts of the Old Testament, including the Deuteronomic History, were compiled for primarily theological reasons, will hardly be disputed. But since the rise
of historical criticism, it has been assumed that theological
insight is to be had first of all through understanding of the
processes by which the texts reached their canonical form, and
through an assessment of the historical veracity of the traditions they present. Recently, it has been questioned whether
this assumption is appropriate to the task, and whether, rather,
the canonical texts should not be approached as integral pieces
of theological literature, whose meaning is to be sought primarily from their inner structure.

0.2   In this chapter, we apply to a part of the Old Testament which has usually been approached by historicizing methods,
other methods drawn from structuralism and literary criticism.

We do so not in a doctrinaire way, for, with Culley (1974: 169), we take structuralism as a suggestive set of methods, rather than as a "philosophical option". These methods have suggested, where others have not, the key significance of Jonathan in the theology of 1 Samuel.

0.3   The first section justifies the scope of the investigation (1 Sam 13-31) and the concentration on the character Jonathan. The second is a close examination of this section, and particularly of the contribution Jonathan makes to it. The third applies a variety of methods to the illumination of the character Jonathan, and hence to the confirming of his significance in these chapters.

1.   The theological problematic of 1 Sam 13-31

1.1   Most commentators find a major division in 1 Sam at the end of ch. 15, seeing either chs. 7-15 or chs. 8-15 as a major section (recently, e.g. Ackroyd, Hertzberg, Stoebe: 1973). An essay by McCarthy (1973) suggests, however, that the major division is after ch. 12. He deals with chs. 8-12, the section on the beginning of kingship in Israel, and, going beyond the numerous theories of different sources in these chapters, sees the whole section as a closely-edited treatment of a severe theological problem: How can a people of whom Yahweh is sole king become a human monarchy under Yahweh? The problem is severe, for the theological legitimacy of the system under which Israel lives is in question. The answer goes roughly like this: Yahweh is Israel's king; for Israel to desire a human king is sinful; Yahweh meets Israel halfway -- after due expiation of the sin, Yahweh looks with favor on the sinful wish, and approves Israel's human king. The firm formal structure of these chapters -- three assemblies of all Israel alternating with two traditional stories about Saul -- proves a very effective vehicle for the theology, but presents a sequence which is the historian's despair, or should be!

1.21   The present paper took its start from our reading McCarthy's, being satisfied with it, and asking, what next? If one problem has been laid to rest, what new one do the following chapters take up? The answer is immediately clear. Monarchy is, from the deuteronomic point of view, dynastic /1/. If Yahweh approved Israel's monarchy, why then do her later

kings not trace their descent from her first king? Why David-
ides, not Saulides? Yahweh swore with David an eternal covenant (2 Sam 7) that one of his descendants would always sit on
his throne, a covenant which even sin could not annul. Did
Yahweh swear such a covenant with Saul? If so, how could it
be annulled? If not, was Saul's kingship real, was Yahweh
"for real" in approving it? Again, the theological stakes are
high, nothing less than the legitimacy of David's line, under
which Israel lives. This problem, we suggest, dominates the
whole rest of the book /2/.

1.22   The section 1 Sam 13-31 is noted for the profusion of
doublets, non sequiturs, and narrative implausibilities which
it contains; this is usually explained as the result of editorial activity (e.g. Weiser, 1961: 159-160). But why is the
editorial work so "poor"? Admittedly we are dealing with canons
of narrative construction of which we have limited understanding, but it seems worth hazarding a different suggestion, that
the narrative problems are a marker of the severity of the
theological problem to be solved.

1.3   The thesis of this paper is that 1 Sam 13-31 is
Israel's theological solution to the theological problem out-
lined; and further, that the character Jonathan is much the
most important of the means of solving (of "mediating", in a
sense to be defined) this problem. The transition from Saul
to David, otherwise theologically implausible, is by Jonathan
made theologically plausible. And we suggest that the testing
of this thesis should assume precedence over attempts to
assess the historicity of the Jonathan traditions, in other
words that he is better approached as a literary character
than as a historical figure.

2.   The character Jonathan in 1 Sam 13-31

2.0   A working structure based on Jonathan's appearances

2.01   The following description of the shape of the section
is a working tool, whose value is to be judged by the insight
it provides. The movement towards David's kingship begins before he even appears, in the account of Saul's rejection. Chs.
13-15 we therefore call preamble. 16:1-13, the secret anointing of David, is a focal scene. Thereafter, sections describing

the relation of David to Saul, and lacking Jonathan, alternate
with sections where Jonathan appears. For present purposes,
we disregard 31:2. The Saul-David sections are usually much
longer than the Jonathan ones (20:1-21:1 is the exception) /3/.
By the fourth Saul-David section (21:2-23:15a) other material
enters in, but their relationship is still the major theme.
After 23:18, it becomes one theme among several, though still
important. It is not merely in a formal sense that the Saul-
David sections lack Jonathan. With the single exception of
22:8, there seems to be nothing in them that would be different if Jonathan did not exist /4/.

2:02   Schematically, the structure is as follows:

                Preamble: The rejection of Saul   chs. 13-15
                Focal scene: The anointing of David   16:1-13
                1st Saul-David section   16:14-17:58
                1st Jonathan section   18:1-5
                2nd Saul-David section   18:6-30
                2nd Jonathan section   19:1-7
                3rd Saul-David section   19:8-24
                3rd Jonathan section   20:1-21:1 /3/
                4th Saul-David section
                        (with other material)   21:2-23:15a
                4th Jonathan section   23:15b-18
                5th Saul-David section
                        (with much other material)   23:19 onward

2.1   The preamble and the focal scene

2.11   The formal rejection of Saul is a prerequisite for
the movement toward David's becoming king. Elsewhere we have
tried to show that chs. 13-15 have the purpose of stating this
formal rejection, and that in particular 14:1-46 depicts Saul
as the rejected king:

                Saul in this story is not so much wicked as fool-
                ish and frustrated. His intentions are good, in-
                deed thoroughly pious, but he pursues them in
                self-defeating ways, and events thwart them . . . .
                The passage presents a skillful portrait of a re-
                jected king, wholly coherent with the rejection
                oracles of chs. 13 and 15. His character and fate
                bear out his rejectedness (Jobling, 1976: 368).

To achieve this portrait, we further suggested, the traditional
view of Saul, mostly positive, has been much altered. But if
14:1-46 shows a tendency in relation to Saul, so it does also
in relation to Jonathan. He receives such marks of divine
approval, and such acclaim of the people, as befits a king, and
does so in the very context of his father's rejection. Our
study concluded as follows:

> We have shown how the redaction of 1 Sam 14:1-46
> tends to diminish Saul and exalt Jonathan. We
> have discussed in detail how this meant the al-
> teration and even reversal of traditions. We
> have suggested that the reader, coming to the
> section aware of Saul's rejection, must ask at
> the end whether Jonathan is not the successor
> appointed by Yhwh.
>
> But, for the attentive reader, this contradicts
> the apparent implication of 13:13-14, that the
> rejection of Saul was the rejection of his dynasty
> too. What, then, can the exaltation of Jonathan
> mean? This question receives no answer in 14:1-46.
> The answer is undoubtedly to be sought in the medi-
> ary role which Jonathan is later to play in the
> transition from Saul's kingship to David's (Jobling,
> 1976: 375-76).

2.12   To this we add a footnote at a more formal level.
The relationship between Saul and Jonathan shows <u>both</u> role-
identification between the two (13:2, 22; 14:21) <u>and</u> replacement of Saul by Jonathan, in the fighting of Saul's battles
(13:3; 14:1-15; cf. 9:16), and in the affection of the people
(14:45). This pattern of identification and replacement /5/
will be extremely important for our further discussion.

2.13   The focal scene, the secret anointing of David, is
reminiscent of the witches' scenes in <u>Macbeth</u>; brief and formal in structure, mysterious in content, and secret, but providing the motive and explanation for the surrounding narrative. David, apparently, knows his destiny from the start,
though the other principals do not.

2.2   The Saul-David sections

2.20   The program of these sections is stated at the

outset. Yahweh has departed from Saul (16:14), but is with
David (16:18; cf. 16:13; 18:14). Saul is rejected, David
elected, and everything in these sections drives this home.
Saul is shown negatively in almost every incident, but even
more he is shown as frustrated -- his plans to harm David are
always turning out to David's advantage, his descent to the
depths is the very cause of David's rise. David is shown
positively /6/, and as successful in what he intends. This
is a first level in the contrast between the rejected and the
elected; in character, bad versus good, in intentions, frustration versus success (cf. Conrad: 68-71; Grønbaek: 110). A
second level is the effect each character has on the relationship between them. Saul, as rejected, is disloyal to David,
and tends to drive him away. David, as elected, is loyal to
Saul, and tends to seek his presence. This sets up a great
tension -- the relationship finds no stability whether they
are together or apart.

2.21   In the first section, 16:14-17:58, Saul accepts David,
and the two become intimate. Within the intimacy, however,
David soon asserts his independence of, and superiority over,
Saul, in the Goliath affair. Not even by the offer of his
armor can Saul gain a share of the credit, for David must re-
ject it (17:38-39).

2.221   The next section, 18:6-30, excellently exemplifies
the structure of the relationship -- Saul ever trying to do
David undeserved harm, but succeeding only in helping him.
The son-in-law motif (18:17-29) deserves particular attention.
Saul offers to David, in turn, two of his daughters as wife,
and David actually marries the second, Michal. It is plausible to see in this a statement of the legitimacy of David's
kingship. Under certain circumstances, to be a king's son-in-
law is to be his legitimate heir; one need think only of the
common fairy-tale ending, "my daughter and half my kingdom" as
the hero's reward on the accomplishment of his task (Propp:
63-64). Perhaps, historically, David's status as Saul's son-
in-law did have something to do with his succession /7/.
Morgenstern (1959) finds evidence for such a system of succession in Edom not long before Saul's time, and builds up
from certain hints in the text (for example, David's demand
in 2 Sam 3:14 for Michal's return) the case that it was precisely under this system that David came to the throne.

2.222   This, however, cannot possibly be the function of
the son-in-law motif in the present narrative, whose point of
view is that kingship passes through the male line. No one is
ever represented as assuming otherwise! Morgenstern's work is
an example of finding the meaning of narrative rather from im-
ported historical data than from implicit literary considerations (cf. Barthes, 1972: 249-254). The motif performs here,
in fact, under the constraint of the overriding theological
agenda, a function not natural to it. According to the account,
Saul's motive in offering his daughters was deceitful from the
start. In the fairy-tale motif, the king's offer, though
fraught with peril, is sincere, so that Saul's deceitfulness
represents an ironic use of the motif /8/. The account serves
the character-portrayal of Saul (and also of David, who has
occasion to show becoming modesty!) as well as fitting the
pattern of frustration and success.

2.23   The same theme continues in the next section, 19:8-
24, for Michal becomes David's ally against Saul. The scene
in vss. 18-24 merits comment. Saul's intention to do David
harm is again frustrated, for his pursuit ends in his deep
humiliation (as Saul's pursuits, after his rejection, always
do -- cf. not only chs. 24 and 26, but also his pursuit of the
Philistines in 14:1-46!) The similarities with 9:1-10:16 are
so striking, above all in the repetition of the proverb "Is
Saul also among the prophets?", that we should regard it as a
satirical recapitulation of the earlier passage. Saul's previous visit to Samuel, and his first experience of prophesying,
showed him as the elected one on his way to the height of
fortune; the recapitulation shows the rejected one far gone
in degradation. Stoebe comments appositely:

> In his possession by the spirit, Saul is not
> empowered for action (10:7), but utterly de-
> prived of power. This is the real point, to
> which the idea of the rescue of David has been
> completely subordinated . . . . The clothes
> which are here torn off are the clothes of a
> king,who now, not only in disgraceful nakedness,
> but stripped likewise of power, lies impotently
> on the ground (1973: 368) /9/.

2.24   On 21:2-23:15a little need be said. Material on
Saul's relationship to David is now broken up by other mater-

ial.   David is glorified as a kind of Robin Hood. He befriends
a priest, while Saul is a slaughterer of priests /10/. And
Saul's intentions against David are, as ever, frustrated; as
the section ends, he has lost control of the oracular ephod,
and David, having possession of it, uses it to frustrate Saul
(on this, excellently, Weiss: 187-188). It is also significant that, in his action against the priests, Saul can find
only a foreigner to support him (22:17-19).

2.25   Similar themes continue after 23:18; but now something new occurs, Saul's acknowledgement of David's coming
kingship (24:20; the doublet 26:25 has only a general blessing). We shall consider this below (4.2).

2.3   The Jonathan sections

2.30   According to Leach (67), "From (1 Sam 18) through to
23 every reference to Jonathan serves to emphasize his role
identification with David. This equation implies that David
ultimately replaces Jonathan as Saul's 'rightful' successor".
This correct insight is only a partial one. The character
Jonathan stands in a twofold relationship, to Saul and to David,
and the two parts have parallel structures. In relation to
Saul, he moves between close identification and an independence which frequently suggests his replacing Saul. In relation to David, he moves between close identification and a
self-emptying into David, a readiness to be replaced by him.
We must demonstrate this twofold pattern of identification
and replacement in detail.

2.31   We have already mentioned (2.12) this pattern between
Saul and Jonathan in chs. 13-14. No identification with David
was possible there, of course; but before going on to the
later Jonathan sections we may note, even in ch. 14, two
Jonathan themes which will find recapitulation in David. First,
Jonathan's single combat (independent of Saul) against the
Philistines is echoed in David's combat with Goliath. Second,
Jonathan's infraction of a food tabu, interpreted by the nar-
rative to his credit, finds a close echo in the account of
David and the priest at Nob (21:2-7) /11/.

2.321   Jonathan's first appearance after ch. 14, in 18:1-5,
is sudden and brief, but in a sense this remarkable passage
(understood along with ch. 14) tells everything that is to be

told about him /12/. It follows David's defeat of Goliath and
reintroduction to Saul, and expounds his relationship to Jonathan
in a beautifully structured way:

Ia (vs. 1) Jonathan establishes identification with
     David: "Jonathan loved him as his own self".

IIa (vs. 2) Saul confirms the identification of
     Jonathan with David by adopting David: he "would
     not let him return to his father's house" /13/.

Ib (vss. 3-4) Jonathan makes David his replacement,
     by handing over to him his clothes and weapons.

IIb (vs. 5) Saul confirms the replacement of Jonathan
     by David, sending David out to fight his battles,
     which Jonathan previously did.

The identification-replacement pattern between Jonathan and
David could not be more effectively exhibited.

2.322   But there is more to say. When we last took leave of
Jonathan, in ch. 14, he was at the high point of his fortunes,
to the extent that the reader might see in him the legitimate
heir, with all the signs of Saul's lost kingship (2.11). At
this level, 18:4 can be read only as an abdication -- it is the
royal garments and the royal weapons that he hands over
(Morgenstern: 322, cf. Thompson: 335; dissenting from this,
Stoebe, 1973: 348). David is now king not only in the secret
counsels of Yahweh, but by the abdication in his favor of the
"acting" king! Taken together, 14:1-46 and 18:1-5 have an inner
significance which runs ahead of the external appearances --
the kingship has passed from Saul to David by the mediation of
Jonathan. The remaining Jonathan sections do little more than
reinforce this.

2.331   In 19:1-7, Jonathan's double role-identification is
very clear. Saul tries to enlist him against David (vs. 1a).
But his identification with David is at once reaffirmed (vs.
1b), and he warns David of Saul's intentions (vss. 2-3).
For the time being, however, this is not at the cost of
Jonathan's unity with his father: "Saul listened to the voice
of Jonathan" (vs. 6). The two act as one in restoring David
to his place as Saul's adopted (cf. 18:2), and Jonathan at
once disappears (vs. 7).

2.332   The heavy theological freight of this passage is the
cause, perhaps, of two infelicities of style. First, the redundant use of "father" and "son" in vss. 1-4 suggests the importance of their identification at the point where it is en-
dangered (for another significant use of "father" and "son",
see below, 4.2). Second, the repetition of the name "Jonathan"
at the end, four times in vss. 6-7 (cf. Stoebe, 1973: 357),
makes clear the importance of Jonathan's mediating role. We
note one further point. There are close parallels, down to
vocabulary and phraseology, between this passage and the final
scene of 14:1-46. In one case, Jonathan is under Saul's death
sentence, in the other, David. Each is saved by an external
mediation, in which Saul acquiesces. Here, once more, David's
experience recapitulates Jonathan's!

2.341   Ch. 20, even more than ch. 14, is Jonathan's chapter.
He appears throughout, sometimes in David's, sometimes in
Saul's, company. In vss. 1-23 he is with David. During Saul's
temporary indisposition (he is naked at Ramah), Jonathan is
presented unmistakably as a king. David enters his presence
(pnym), and we are made to think of the royal "presence" of
Saul which David enters and leaves (16:21, 22; 17:57; 19:7).
Jonathan speaks as a king: "Far from it, you shall not die"
(cf. 19:6!) The role identification Saul-Jonathan is tremen-
dously strong in the first verses: "Behold, my father does
nothing either great or small without disclosing it to me" (vs.
2) /14/. The following verses (4-11), display great subtlety.
Even while acting as king, Jonathan strongly affirms his identification with David (vs. 4), and allows himself to be enlist-
ed as mediator. David at first seems to accept the identification of Jonathan with Saul, regarding the son as the father's
plenipotentiary (vs. 8b), and adopting the attitude of a sup-
pliant (vs. 8a, cf. Hertzberg: 172). But David's hints that
Jonathan might act against him elicit a forceful denial: "Far
be it from you!" (vs. 9). The remainder of the passage, vss.
12-23, moves entirely in the identification-replacement pattern
of Jonathan and David. Jonathan's abdication is clear: "May
Yahweh be with you, as he has been with my father" (vs. 13),
and he appeals to be identified with David the coming king.

2.342   In 20:1-23 we witness a great collision between the
Saul-Jonathan pattern of identification and replacement and
the Jonathan-David pattern of identification and replacement.
Perhaps even more plainly than in 14:1-46 and 18:1-5, kingship

passes from Saul to David by means of Jonathan; it is when
Jonathan has most clearly "become king" that he most clearly
"abdicates"!

2.343   20:24-34 finds Jonathan with Saul. Implying the
Jonathan-David identification, Saul questions Jonathan about
David (vs. 27). Implying the Saul-Jonathan identification,
Jonathan replies (vs. 28) that David requested something of
him as of a king (Saul's deputy!) But Saul is not bluffed.
"You have chosen the son of Jesse" (always a pejorative appel-
ation, Stoebe, 1973: 388) " . . . to the shame of your mother's
nakedness", and while David lives "neither you nor your kingdom
shall be established" (vss. 30-31). In this, the only use of
a mlk word in connection with Jonathan, Saul simultaneously
affirms the point of view of the narrative, that kingship is
dynastic, and "forgets" the terms of the oracle of rejection
in 13:13-14, which applied to his whole house /15/. Jonathan
falls into his accustomed role of mediation (vs. 32), which
Saul rejects not by word, but by deed. In one of the most re-
vealing verses (33) of the whole narrative, and without narrative logic, Saul tries to impale Jonathan (Jonathan's experience now recapitulating David's in 18:11 and 19:10!) and
from this Jonathan deduces that his father seeks David's life.
The identification of Jonathan and David is total -- an act
directed at one is an act directed at the other /16/.

2.344   20:35-21:1 sees Jonathan back with David, and partly
recapitulates vss. 1-23. David treats Jonathan as a king,
doing obeisance (vs. 41), and they reaffirm their covenant
identification.

2.35   The last brief passage, 23:15b-18, provides a neat
counterpoint to the last; Jonathan goes out to David as to a
king, reversing 20:1. The identifications are present:
Jonathan's acknowledgement of David is also Saul's ("my father
also knows this"); and Jonathan again appeals to his past relation with David ("I shall be next to you"). But they are
swallowed up in the completeness of the replacement, which is
unambiguous: "You shall be king over Israel".

3.   Approaches to the character Jonathan

3.0   We shall adopt three approaches, two based on structuralist models, the third on a more general literary model.

3.1   An "actantial" model for 1 Sam 13-31

3.11   Greimas (1966: 172-91) has suggested an "actantial schema" by means of which narrative can be analyzed according to its participants, or "actants" (anglicizing the identical French), who need not be people, and their relationship to the movement of the narrative, as follows:

Sender ⟶ Object ⟶ Receiver
           ↑
Helper ⟶ Subject ⟵ Opponent

The <u>sender</u> brings the action about, with the aim of getting the <u>object</u> to the <u>receiver</u>. The <u>subject</u> is the protagonist of the action, which is aided and opposed by various <u>helpers</u> and <u>opponents</u>.

3.12   The actantial scheme which we propose for 1 Sam 13-31 is

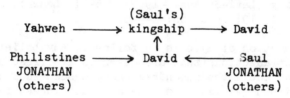

                  (Saul's)
Yahweh ⟶ kingship ⟶ David
               ↑
Philistines ⟶ David ⟵ Saul
JONATHAN   JONATHAN
(others)   (others)

It is the categories "helper" and "opponent" which claim special attention.

3.13   To digress briefly, the placing of the Philistines is most interesting. Historically, it is likely that although they were responsible for Saul's downfall their threat was also the major cause of his rise; and that he enjoyed considerable successes against them. In our chapters, none of this ambiguity is preserved. The Philistines in their every appearance assist the narrative's movement towards David's takeover -- even the accounts of the victories over them in chs. 13-14, for these are Jonathan's, not Saul's! David's successes against the Philistines advance him at Saul's expense. Saul's attempt to use the Philistines to destroy David misfires (18:20-29). The Philistines recognize David's kingship early in the story (21:11). And they prevent his participation in the disastrous final battle (ch. 29), from which, whatever the outcome, he could

have gained no credit in Israel. Greimas's model shows this
consistent function of the Philistines in relation to the aim of
the narrative, even where their activities seem to make poor
historical sense.

3.14   Jonathan, by his mere existence, is the opponent of
the action. He is heir to the throne, so that David must re-
place not only a legitimate monarch, but also a legitimate
heir. But in all his appearances after ch. 14 he is, in action
and word, the helper of the action -- he saves David's life,
tries to maintain his high position in Saul's court, and as it
were hands over the future to David. And when his function is
performed, he disappears, in each instance, quite abruptly.
Greimas's scheme alerts us to this extraordinary ambiguity of
the character Jonathan in relation to the theological problematic.

3.2   Jonathan as mediator

3.20   We here consider the work of Lévi-Strauss on myth,
especially as it has been applied to the Old Testament by Leach
(for the following, Lévi-Strauss, 1963: 206-31; Leach: especially 7-11; Lane: 13-19; Jacobson: 149-57).

3.21   The function of myth is as follows. Any belief system contains contradictions that are essentially irresoluble;
for instance, how could the human race have descended from the
first parents without violation of the absolute incest tabu?
Myths soften, or "mediate", such contradictions, by making it
appear that they are resolved, though they never are. For it
is vital to a society that its belief not appear to be based
on contradictions. In the enormous variety of myths within
societies and across societies, it is the same essential problems which are at issue.

3.22   Belief systems, in other words, abound in binary oppositions (Leach: 9-10; Lane: 16), life and death, endogamy
and exogamy, etc., which are not capable of final resolution.
A characteristic of the myths which mediate them is redundancy,
the saying of the same thing in many different mythical ways:

> Any particular myth in isolation is like a coded
> message badly snarled up with noisy interference.
> Even the most confident devotee might feel a
> little uncertain as to what precisely is being

said. But, as a result of redundancy, the be-
liever can feel that, even when the details
vary, each alternative version of a myth confirms his understanding and reinforces the
essential meaning of all the others (Leach: 9).

The underlying agenda of a myth is its deep structure (Lane: 14-
16), as opposed to the surface structure, that is, its narrated
form(s). In their surface structure, myths are diachronic --
they tell stories in which the passage of time is an element.
But their deep structure is synchronic -- they express relationships within a belief system which need not take any particular view of the time element. The priority of synchrony over
diachrony is characteristic of structuralism: "History is seen
as the specific mode of development of a particular system,
whose present, or synchronic nature must be fully known before
any account can be given of its evolution, or diachronic
nature" (Lane: 17).

3.23   Leach (25-31) has challenged Lévi-Strauss's insistence that his methods are not appropriate for the Old Testament. Boldly applying the term "myth" to his material, Leach
presents the accounts of the struggles over the succession to
David as a mediation between principles of endogamy and exogamy
in Israel (25-83). In what follows, we certainly go beyond
Leach's intentions, for he is still working with themes of
direct concern rather to the anthropologist than to the theo-
logian. Without implying acceptance of his view of the nature
of the deuteronomic narrative, we make use of a method which
has been suggested by his.

3.24   The theological problematic discovered in 1 Sam 8-12
by McCarthy (see 1.1) may be readily expressed in binary form:

1. Human monarchy is alien to Yahwism, but
2. Israel is a human monarchy under Yahweh.

So, likewise, may the problematic of the succeeding chapters:

1. Monarchy is inherently dynastic, but
2. Israel's monarchy is not traced from her
    first king.

This opposition Jonathan mediates. In a dynastic system, the

only way in which an outsider may legitimately succeed is as a
result of an abdication. For reasons to be considered (cf.
4.1), Saul cannot abdicate in David's favor, and this means
an impasse. But what he cannot himself do, perhaps he can do
in the person of his legitimate heir. At least, this is the
best way available out of the impasse. Jonathan's identification with, his heirdom to, Saul, provide him with the royal
authority to abdicate; his identification with David enables
the emptying of his own heirdom into David.

3.25   Other structuralist categories provide insight into
the narrative. The use of Jonathan certainly exhibits redundancy. All that is essential is in 14:1-46 and 18:1-5 (cf.
2.321-322), but there follow three more Jonathan sections;
that is, sections where the theological problem can only be
broached alternate with ones in which it is "resolved". To
speak of redundancy is to stress the synchronic. Although
the Jonathan sections do exhibit diachrony (e.g. Jonathan's
declarations of David's coming kingship grow in clarity, 18:4;
20:13-16; 23:17), synchrony is at least equally clear; a good
example is David's obeisance to Jonathan in 20:41, recalling
vss. 1-11 and making little sense "after" Jonathan's declaration in vss. 13-16.

3.26   As to deep structure, we have already pursued the
implications of the Jonathan sections below the narrative
level. But may we not go deeper, and suggest that we see
here a manifestation of one of the most basic of biblical
oppositions, that between divine demand and divine grace, or
between the conditional and the unconditional covenant? Between these there is in the Old Testament not a static choice
but an ultimately irresoluble conflict; Yahweh's grace is
utterly free, Yahweh's demand is utterly binding. Saul sins,
and must be rejected. But Yahweh made him a promise, which
must be kept. Therefore, the passing of Saul's kingship
must express the radical discontinuity caused by sin (the
kingship is torn from him), but also the radical continuity
guaranteed by grace -- the kingship passes by legitimate
means to one who has become his heir.

3.3   Character and plot

3.31   Scholes and Kellogg make these statements about
ancient narrative: "As in the epic, character in the saga is

conceived in terms of plot. In this perfectly self-contained
narrative world, the characters are not endowed with any
attributes extraneous to the action being presented" (173),
and "Characters in primitive stories are invariably 'flat,'
'static,' and quite 'opaque'" (164). Apparently, however,
they do not intend to include the Old Testament in such judg-
ments, for elsewhere they contrast it with Greek literature:

> The heroes of the Old Testament were in a pro-
> cess of becoming, whereas the heroes of Greek
> narrative were in a state of being. Process in
> Greek narrative was confined to the action of a
> plot. And even so, the action exemplified un-
> changing, universal laws; while the agents of
> the action, the characters, became as the plot
> unfolded only more and more consistent ethical
> types. Abraham, Jacob, David, and Samson, on
> the other hand, are men whose personal develop-
> ment is the focus of interest (123).

We suggest, however, that in our section character _is_ very much
subordinate to plot; not, perhaps, because character is unim-
portant, but because _here_ plot, the theological agenda, is
overwhelmingly important.

3.321   Before discussing Jonathan, it is instructive to consider the two major protagonists, Saul and David. They show
character traits, and appear to act from discernible motives.
Saul acts to keep the kingship for himself and his house.
But here two difficulties arise. First, why should he do so,
having been plainly told that kingship will depart from him
and his house (13:13-14)? Second, why does he do so so badly,
in such consistently self-defeating ways? David, on the other
hand, in the usual (historicizing) view, early sets his sights
on the kingship, and pursues it with patience and opportunism.
But why should he do so, having been already anointed king?

3.322   It seems accurate to say that even in Saul and David
character is almost entirely (making allowances for the
strength of tradition and the exigencies of story-telling) in
the service of plot. Saul is rejected, David elected, and the
character and experience of each bears out that rejection and
that election; must bear them out, for the success of the narrative. The rejected is bad, the elected is good, and to ask

after cause and effect is pointless. The rejected is frustrated by events (so that his bad acts turn out for good!),
while the elected is advanced by events.

3.33   Jonathan is the extreme case of character emptied
into plot; at least after ch. 14 /17/ he is flat, static, and
certainly opaque (3.31), his attitudes and actions lacking
any normal motivation. He is the heir, and the heir does not
normally champion the cause of an upstart against his own.
Morgenstern's view, that Jonathan accepted the custom of son-
in-law succession, we have already rejected (2.222; one may
reasonably doubt whether there is any traditio-historical link,
in any case, between Michal and Jonathan). Psychologizing
solutions are suggested particularly by Hertzberg: "On Jonathan's
side (the friendship with David) is completely disinterested"
(154), and "In the figure of Jonathan, the Old Testament has a
real nobleman of high sensibility" (172). It is one thing,
however, to show even an extreme case of a human virtue, but
quite another to act without reason against oneself! Jonathan
after ch. 14 is so lacking in features that might grow out of
traditions about him that one is forced to wonder whether
there were any such traditions, whether he is not a purely
literary construction.

3.341   Conrad (67) finds a motivation for Jonathan from
another direction; he takes the initiative on David's side
"not only out of human love and attachment, but above all because it becomes known to him . . . that this is Yahweh's
chosen, and he acknowledges this (20:13ff.; 23:16f.)". This
hardly means that Jonathan "saw which way the wind was blowing"
and acted opportunistically, for on more than one occasion
he could have allowed David to be killed simply by doing
nothing. Rather, he came to know the divine plan, and acted
in accordance with it. The theme of knowledge, of who knows
what is going on in the narrative, is a very important and
also a very problematic one, requiring a separate study /18/,
but we must sketch the problem. As a pointer, we may quote
Hertzberg (156), speaking of Saul's first mistrust of David:
"Anyone who knows how events are to turn out, of course, knows
the deeper justification of his mistrust: David is really
destined to be Saul's successor". On the face of it, this
statement is meaningless, for what has the narrator's knowledge of the outcome to do with Saul's mistrust? But such
knowledge is pivotal for the narrative.

3.342   David is made privy to the theological agenda at his
anointing, and his knowledge of what Yahweh is doing never
becomes a major issue /19/. Saul does not learn who his successor is, but he does learn of the rejection of his house, so
that ignorance of this on his part is refusal to know. Leach
(67) notes that the narrative makes Saul, rather than David,
the rebel; and wherein can Saul's rebellion against Yahweh lie
but in this refusal to know? It is tempting to find a marker
of this "epistemological" rebellion in Samuel's words to Saul:
"Rebellion is as the sin of divination" (15:23). The one who
refuses to know by direct prophetic oracle (13:13-14) seeks to
know by witches (ch. 28)!

3.343   Jonathan receives no revelations, and yet he knows.
Mysteriously, the divine plan is open to him. His discern-
ment is clear enough even in 20:13-16, but in 23:17 he speaks
to David as a prophet speaks: "The hand of my father shall
not find you; you shall be king over Israel, and I shall be
next to you."

3.35   In his reckless courage, his mysterious insight into events, his utterly selfless surrender of himself to this
insight, who are Jonathan's literary counterparts? In different ways, we may perhaps look to Perceval, to Dostoevsky's
Idiot, even to Don Quixote. Like Myshkin, "He was an ideal
character, a God's fool" (Gibson: 105, and cf. Welsford: 88-
112, on the clairvoyant fools of Ireland). His motivation is
Yahweh's motivation, ultimately unknown. His initiative on
David's behalf (Conrad: 67) is Yahweh's initiative. He has,
as Hertzberg (193) instinctively discerns, one notable biblical counterpart in John the Baptist, in whom the old age
recognizes and yields to the new.

4.   Conclusions

4.0   From this investigation we attempt a summary statement of the role of Jonathan in 1 Sam 13-31. These chapters
must make theologically acceptable the transition from Saul's
kingship to David's. We are concerned not with how this took
place historically, and for what reasons, but rather with the
answers given in the text, and coherent with its implicit
point of view. Saul's incapacity to rule does not legitimize
David (cf. Grønbaek: 119). Nor does any amount of support

from various individuals and factions (Grønbaek: 273). Nor
does being Saul's son-in-law, though in another frame of
reference it would (2.222).

4.1   The Saul-David sections through 23:15a work well in
their own terms. They depict the rejected one as bad and
appropriately rejected, the elected one as good and appropriately elected. They create superb narrative tension in the
interplay between Saul's disloyalty to David and David's
loyalty to Saul. But these sections cannot show David's
legitimacy, and do not try. David can be king only if Saul
gives place to him. But Saul cannot give place to David and
still "be himself" -- this would call for knowledge of Yahweh's
plan and obedience to it. These the rejected one cannot have;
his lack of them goes along with his rejection!

4.2   The impossibility of solving the theological problem
by means of Saul and David alone is shown after 23:19; for
here the attempt is apparently made to do so (perhaps a relic
of a stage of the tradition which lacked the Jonathan sections) /20/. The attempt is made, that is, to show Saul both
as the rejected one and as willingly abdicating to David. In
ch. 24, he begins by seeking David's life, and ends by con-
fessing David's future kingship (vs. 20). Their next encoun-
ter, in ch. 26, is a "redundant" repetition of this cycle,
though without the specific confession. Noteworthy in these
chapters is the frequent use of "father" and "son" (24:11, 16;
26:17, 21, 25; cf. above, 2.332). But in the very next verse
(27:1) David complains of the continuing danger to his life
from Saul. The attempt fails; the theological aim is here
pursued at the cost of narrative coherence, and even of psychological conviction; at no level does the account make sufficient sense.

4.3   The introduction of Jonathan appears at first to add
to the problems; David must now supplant not only a king, but
a legitimate heir. But this is illusory; Jonathan will die
with Saul, since Saul's house is rejected. Meanwhile, Jonathan provides what is needed. As Saul's heir, he has the
kingly power to abdicate; as separate from Saul, he can do so
without disrupting Saul's character-portrayal. David can receive Jonathan's armor (18:4) where he cannot receive Saul's
(17:38-39)! The theological aim is pursued first by a beauti-
ful technique of interlacing the Jonathan sections with the

Saul-David sections; again and again we are put in touch with
the resolution of the problem which the Saul-David sections
necessarily leave unresolved. Second, Jonathan's mediation of
the theological problem is signalled by his mediation between
Saul and David at the narrative level. Third, at the deeper
level, and coming to the surface in a variety of ways, are the
structural patterns which bear the burden of the theology, the
double pattern of identification and replacement between Saul
and Jonathan and between Jonathan and David.

4.4   The narrators worked with a theological paradox, ad-
mitting no "solution". We may admire their skill, though we
cannot know the extent to which the phenomena we have studied
were consciously intended. But a judgment on their "success"
is meaningless. That their work was a <u>sufficient</u> treatment
of the paradox is demonstrated simply by its survival as
sacred scripture /21/.

FOOTNOTES TO CHAPTER I

/1/   The problematic question, whether the historical Saul
expected to found a dynasty, is irrelevant here. On 13:13-14,
cf. Grønbaek: 125.

/2/   Weiser (1966: 354) sees the account of David's rise
as a "tendentious work . . . which, though it arranges diverse
traditions of unequal historical value in chronological order,
sees its goal as the divine legitimation of (the rule of) King
David and his dynasty over Israel . . . " (the article contains
numerous details of how this goal was pursued).

/3/   References here and throughout are to the Masoretic
chapter and verse divisions, which differ in ch. 21 from those
of the English translations (21:2 = English 21:1, etc.).

/4/   On the possibility that the Jonathan traditions were
originally separate, cf. 4.2.

/5/   Of the interplay between the identification and the
separation of Saul and Jonathan, the two lots in 14:40-42 provide a neat parable -- first the two together over against the
people, then the two over against each other!

/6/   A negative view of David is perhaps implied in 21:2-7
(his misrepresentation of the facts to Ahimelech), or in ch.
25 (his intended violence against Nabal's house, not carried
out). But even these are readily to be understood under the
rubric that everything turns out for the best for him. By
no means is there anything negative about David in ch. 22 --
Saul's words (vss. 7-8) simply confirm the king's vindictive-
ness, and David's own (vs. 22) show him truly penitent over
consequences of his action which were scarcely his fault. Any
negative hints in the account of David's rise are put in perspective when contrasted with the "realistic" and damning
account of his actions towards Uriah (2 Sam 11).

/7/   On the extraordinary complexity of the traditions
involved, cf. Stoebe, 1961; Grønbaek: 104-109.

/8/   Grønbaek (104-105) suggests that, in the tradition,
Saul may have had positive intentions in offering Michal.

/9/   Grønbaek (119-20) sees the incident as fictional,
composed precisely as an expression of Saul's rejectedness,
and further to confirm David's legitimacy (but cf. 4.0). On
the crux between 15:35 and 19:18-24 (Samuel does see Saul
again) it is best to conclude that this is one of the narrative tensions occasioned by the theological urgency of showing Saul rejected.

/10/   On Saul's relationship with the house of Eli, cf.
Jobling, 1976: 368-69. In ch. 14, he is only hindered by the
Elide priest, and his very association with a rejected house
(cf. 2:27-36) is a further indication that his own house is
rejected. The scene in 22:11-19 thus lies on two axes of
divine rejection.

/11/   We owe this suggestion to D. J. McCarthy.

/12/   The absence of this section, and of large parts of
ch. 17, from the LXX, we here ignore, despite its importance
for historical investigation. Our present purpose is literary
investigation of the Hebrew text.

/13/   Some scholars see vs. 2 as inserted into the immediate context, being the original conclusion to 17:55-58 (Grønbaek: 92; de Vries: 27-28; dissenting, Stoebe, 1973: 347-48).

If this is correct, it makes the subsequent structuring of vss.
1-5 only the more striking.

/14/   Hertzberg speaks of "Jonathan, who imagines himself
to be in full possession of his father's confidence" (172).
This psychological interpretation is too shallow to account
for Jonathan's formal declaration.

/15/   For reasons which are not clear, Stoebe (1973: 389)
regards it as impossible (in 20:31 and 23:17) to see Jonathan
as regarding himself as heir apparent, but as giving up his
claim and taking second place. Perhaps he has in mind simply
the historical implausibility (cf. 3.33).

/16/   The spear is cast "in effect at David" (Stoebe, 1973:
288).

/17/   It is not clear whether there is significance in the
orthographic change in Jonathan's name (yō- in chs. 13-14, except 14:6, 8; yᵉhō- in 14:6, 8 and after ch. 17).

/18/   Such a study would need to take account of the pre-
valence of the theme of ignorance even at the surface level:
e.g. Saul's ignorance of what is going on in ch. 14; his having to ask who David is after the fight with Goliath (17:55-58;
for a summary of attempts to deal with this famous crux, and
a new suggestion, Willis: 295-302); his "no one tells me
anything" (22:8).

/19/   Historically correct, no doubt, but nonetheless quite
facile, is Hertzberg's remark: "For the further course of this
history the anointing remains, of course, without importance"
(139).

/20/   Conrad (66-67) seems to suggest this.

/21/   For clarity of focus, we have left unconsidered any
other theological significance of Jonathan than in relation to
the major theological problem of the section. The reincor-
poration of the tribe of Benjamin into a Davidic monarchy,
which becomes a problem in 2 Sam, is already prepared for here
(cf. 20:15 and 23:17 in particular). This problem is eased if
it is accepted that Saul's troubles came from Yahweh, that his
family assisted David, and above all that Jonathan's non-
succession was volitional.

Chapter II

A Structural Analysis of Numbers 11-12

> . . . it is necessary to take the chapters
> Num 11 and 12 together in their entirety
> when making an analysis (Noth, 1972: 128).
>
> . . . our aim will be to start with the
> myth . . . considered as a narrative unity,
> trying to make explicit the descriptive pro-
> cedures necessary to attain, by successive
> stages, the maximum "readability" (lisibilité
> maximale) of this myth (Greimas, 1970: 186).

0.   Introduction

0.1   Num 11-12 consists of three sections, 11:1-3, 11:4-35,
and ch. 12, clearly delineated by locale and by the closure of
the incident in each. The second of these sections, moreover,
tells of two events which superficially are only loosely connected: the quail (11:4-9, 10*, 13, 18-24a, 31-34), and the
elders (11:10*, 11-12, 14-17, 24b-30) -- the status of the dif-
ficult vs. 10 will be discussed below. Yet the two chapters
have not proved amenable to source-analysis, and many inter-
relationships among the parts invite us to follow Noth (1972:
128) in regarding them as a unit at some stage of the "literary
elaboration" of the traditions. Most important among these are
the themes of leadership and prophecy, the locations of tent of
meeting, camp, and outside the camp, and, at the lexicographi-
cal level, the recurrence of the roots ʾsp ("gather") and ʾkl
("eat, consume" , usually in combination with bśr, "meat, flesh").
Numerous other connections will be dealt with in what follows.

0.2   The chosen text will be considered as a <u>system</u>, both
narratively and semantically (see 0.3), for the carrying of a
message. We shall seek to lay bare this system. Such an en-
terprise is to be judged by, among other means, its success in
accounting for the <u>details</u> of the text, so that the analysis
is necessarily intricate. A methodological problem involved
in an analysis of one section of biblical narrative is the relation of text to context. Our text is part of a larger system, and we are aware of the necessity of extending the investigation (see 4). Our beginning with a sub-system can be
justified only by its results. From time to time we shall in-
voke the larger system (of the Pentateuch), e.g. to determine
what understanding the reader of Num 11-12 is to have of leprosy laws (1.1142), or of the location of the tent of meeting
(2.2311). In doing this, we consider only the final form of
the literature, not its history of development, so that sections whose traditions are no doubt older are still to be read
in relation to ones whose traditions are no doubt younger. We
shall make no assumptions about what authors or redactors <u>in-
tended</u> to say. We are working at a level of analysis at which
the <u>text</u> is abstracted, so far as possible, from its history
and from its authorship. This is necessary only at a preliminary stage of the work; at a later stage there must be inter-
action with the findings of traditional historical-critical
methods.

0.3   We shall follow in our analysis the examples of
D. Patte (1976) and J. Calloud (1976a and b), who both apply to
biblical texts the methods of A. J. Greimas. In particular, we
shall divide the work into two large sections, <u>narrative</u> analysis (1) and <u>semantic</u> analysis (2). This is to make a conscious
separation (though it cannot be an ultimate distinction) between the two aspects of structural analysis inspired respectively by V. Propp, the search for the structure of narrative
<u>as such</u>, and C. Lévi-Strauss, the search for meaning in the
discrete elements of narrative. In the first part we shall
analyze <u>stories</u> -- the whole unit as a single story, and the
sub-stories of which it is made. At a second stage we shall
analyze the meaning-effects of our texts under its major isotopies and codes (for the terminology, e.g. Crespy: 32-36;
Greimas, 1966: 69-70; 1970: 189-197, and passim in his work;
Lévi-Strauss, 1969: 199). These two terms do not greatly
differ in meaning; both refer to "headings" under which many
elements of meaning in a text may be usefully gathered. But

"code" refers to an existing human system of classification, (e.g. a cosmology), "isotopy" to a more general or abstract idea (e.g. the supernatural). The presentation of the analysis is necessarily iterative, that is, conclusions of later parts are anticipated in the presentation of earlier parts (cf. e.g. 2.2, on the order of introduction of the codes). One aims at the most effective presentation, but all the parts must be judged from the whole. At each stage of analysis there are residues, textual elements which have been bracketed out while the system of other elements was being displayed. These residues become then the objects of later stages of analysis. But even after our analysis residues remain (cf. especially 2.225), for a textual analysis, like a psychoanalysis, never ends (Lévi-Strauss, 1969: 5)!

0.4   The "results" or "exegetical gains" of structural biblical analyses tend at present to be modest. We are still at the stages of observation of structural phenomena, and of elementary organization of them, rather than of interpretation. Attempts should be judged as much by the ground they stake out as by that which they securely gain! Our study does have implications for detailed exegesis (e.g. Moses' statement in 11:29, "Would that all Yahweh's people were prophets", is judged negatively by the narrative). But our real interest is in the viability, for the further study of biblical narrative, of the story-typologies of 1.1, of the suggestions in 1.2 about the structural constraints on "redaction", and of the system for the organization of meaning-effects in 2 (cf. the summary table in 2.3).

1.   Narrative analysis

1.0   We shall employ the following sigla for the stories delineated above (0.1):

> SA   11:1-3
> SB   The quail story
> SC   The elders story
> SD   Ch. 12

The narrative analysis will in its turn be divided into two parts, paradigmatic and syntagmatic (e.g. Culler: 44-48) /1/. That is, we shall study the four stories first in parallel,

for their structural similarities one to another, and then as
the unified whole which they now present.

1.1   Paradigmatic narrative analysis

1.11   The surface logic of the stories

1.110   The paradigmatic analysis begins with an endeavour to
uncover the logic of each of the four stories, to suggest what
they are getting at even where they speak unclearly, to fill
lacunae and draw out unstated implications. This uncovering
of the logic is hazardous and uncertain, and turns, in extreme
cases, into the imposing of a logic which the text does not
clearly imply, but which it does not preclude. "It would not
be possible to perform a structural analysis by studying a non-
deciphered [text]" (Calloud, 1976b: 11). But even here the procedure is iterative (0.3) -- our choices reflect, in a few
cases, the later analysis.

1.111   SA (Num 11:1-3)

           The first, brief story presents few problems. The
object of the people's complaint is unspecified, but we shall
argue that it is against the wilderness journey as such (1.121).
They complain "in the hearing of Yahweh", but this means his
"overhearing" rather than their attempt to communicate with
him (2.1221). Nothing here suggests that Yahweh considers ex-
terminating the people (though the larger narrative raises
this possibility, 14:12, Ex 32:10); he seeks to stop the complaining. In the end, the status quo is reestablished, except
for the remaining effects of Yahweh's fire.

1.112   SB (the quail story)

1.1121   By itself, the outer framework of this story (vss.
4-9, 31-34) would be fairly coherent at the surface level.
Moses is absent. There are two groups of complainants in vs.
4, the "rabble" (using the RSV word for convenience; on the
significance of ʾspsp, see 2.2312), and the "people of Israel".
The rabble's "craving" is unspecified, but presumably it is
for meat. Vs. 34 differentiates between the "people" and the
"craving people", only the latter dying from the "blow" (mkh)
of Yahweh in vs. 33. These must be precisely the "rabble" of
vs. 4 (so Coats: 111), and we shall hereafter use "rabble" and

"people" strictly to define the two groups /2/. The picture is
that the rabble seek not merely to satisfy their own appetite,
but instigate the people to join in their complaining. Yahweh,
for reasons that are not clear, provides meat, but, before anyone can eat it, kills the rabble. The aims of Yahweh's activity
seem to be, to separate the people from the rabble, to kill
the rabble, and to keep the people from eating meat. By burying the rabble (vs. 34), the people themselves set the seal on
the separation. The status quo is restored, except that the
rabble no longer exists to threaten it.

1.1122   The middle section, in which Moses appears, greatly
complicates this coherent picture. The main problem is that
he has already told the people (vs. 24a) that the "gift" of
quail will in fact be a punishment (vss. 19-20). This makes
their gathering of the quail into an outright ignoring of
Yahweh's word, and Yahweh's saving of them from the consequences an unaccountable act of grace (in this story, the
"people" are never punished at all!). Logic seems to demand
(and vs. 23 makes plausible) that the sending of the quail is
a demonstration of Yahweh's power to Moses /3/, from the consequences of which the people are then protected by a special
measure. If this hypothesis is correct, the weight of SB is
heavily on the character Moses.

1.1123   Moses is here Yahweh's antagonist (as the intertwining of SB with SC will confirm). According to the wording of
vs. 10, Moses is displeased not merely with the people's complaint, but with the whole situation, including Yahweh's anger.
In vs. 13, he (i) accepts the people's demand for meat, ignoring the implication (vss. 5-6) that their real desire is to
return to Egypt; (ii) assumes that it is his responsibility to
meet the demand, even claiming that the people have made it
directly to him; and (iii) expresses his inability to do what
is demanded. Yahweh's reply (vss. 18-20) turns aside all of
these points, (i) exposing the rebellion implied in the people's
demand; (ii) treating the demand as directed to himself, and
ignoring any role for Moses except that of announcing the divine intention; and (iii) announcing his own ability to provide more than is demanded. Moses expresses his doubts on the
last point with unconcealed irony (vss. 21-22, still implying
a considerable role for himself in any provision of meat).

1.1124   After we learn of Yahweh's anger at the people's
complaint (vs. 10), we expect his punishment of them (cf. vs.

1), and such punishment is apparently announced in vss. 19-20.
That it never comes may be explained by the shift in the interest of the text from the people's rebellion to Moses'
doubts. Such an explanation no doubt correctly locates the
main concern of the story; but it does not solve the problem
at the deepest level. If the story does not <u>record</u> a punishment of the people, it is because its exigencies do not <u>re-
quire</u> one. We shall return (1.1222) to this significant
question.

1.113   SC (the elders story)

1.1131   Moses is here, from the outset, Yahweh's antagonist,
complaining about the <u>status quo</u>, that is, his unique role as
leader /4/. Yahweh apparently complies with Moses' request
for aid, but the narrative takes several baffling turns, and
reaches, at the surface level, no satisfactory conclusion.
First, the elders do not share Moses' leadership. They share
his spirit of prophecy, but this cannot be an empowerment for
leadership ("bearing the burden of the people"), since neither
in this passage nor in the larger narrative do we hear anything
of their sharing Moses' office. Second, even their prophecy
ends as soon as it has begun /5/, so that the whole matter of
the 70 elders comes to nothing at all. Third, however, there
are outside the main group of 70 two <u>named</u> individuals, Eldad
and Medad. Although they were apparently part of the group
chosen by Moses, they remain in the camp while the others go
to the tent of meeting. And their prophesying is different
from that of the 70 -- it is not Moses', but Yahweh's, spirit
that rests on them (vs. 29), and their prophesying is not
said to <u>cease</u> (cf. the rabbinic tradition in 3.3 below). This
story does not end in the restoration of the <u>status quo</u>, but
rather, in the figures of Eldad and Medad, reaches an ambiguous conclusion.

1.1132   Moses seeks his own diminishment, and he does suffer
a diminishment /6/, but not a great nor necessarily a permanent
one. His request, which Yahweh has promised to fulfil, leads
to (i) no more than a passing incident in the case of the main
body of elders, and (ii) an unclear issue in the case of just
Eldad and Medad. And prophecy, the text surely implies, is a
lesser thing that "bearing the burden of the people" (2.123).
We suggest that Yahweh, in his apparently favourable response
to the request, gives Moses himself such a role in the carrying

out of it that he cannot fulfil this role without eviscerating
the request! Moses is himself to choose the elders and gather
them to the tent (vs. 16). But if he is uniquely able to
choose the best candidates, and if he obediently does his part,
is he not tacitly carrying out the unique leadership role
against which he complained? That the story is affirming
Moses' uniqueness precisely at the moment of its "dissipation"
is hinted at by the otherwise inexplicable note that Yahweh
singles Moses out for a conversation, of undisclosed content,
immediately before the distribution of the spirit (vs. 25,
"and spoke to him", cf. vs. 17)!

1.1133   In the case of the 70, Moses carries out his instructions precisely, and the sharing of his leadership quickly
comes to nothing. In the case of Eldad and Medad something
goes wrong, which, in the terms of the story, can only mean
that Moses failed to carry out his instructions precisely --
he chose Eldad and Medad, but did not gather them to the tent.
So Yahweh endows them with his own spirit (cf. vs. 29), implying a much more real threat to Moses' unique position. And
still Moses responds to this in the terms of his initial desire for shared responsibility, carrying it, indeed, to an extreme: "Would that all Yahweh's people were prophets" (vs. 29).
As the story ends, the irregular activity of Eldad and Medad,
not mediated through Moses, still disturbs the status quo.

1.114   SD (Num 12)

1.1141   Miriam and Aaron challenge Moses' unique position on
the ground that they, as well as he, are prophets (Yahweh
speaks through them). The fact that, in vs. 1, Miriam is mentioned first, and that only she is punished, has suggested to
many interpreters that she instigated the affair and persuaded
Aaron to join her. Otherwise, there is no ready explanation
for the different treatment of Miriam and Aaron. Aaron indeed
repents, and is not punished; but Miriam's punishment is not
due to her lack of repentance, for she has no opportunity before the blow falls. The narrative stresses the separation
which Yahweh makes between the offenders, and draws particular attention to Aaron's penitence, intercession for Miriam,
and submission to Moses (to whom, rather than to Yahweh, he
addresses his appeal, vss. 11-12). At the end of the story,
the status quo is restored, except for the punishment, or
marking, of Miriam.

1.1142   We tentatively suggest that Miriam's punishment can
be illumined by examination of the laws concerning leprosy in
Leviticus; there is, at least, very ancient precedent for bring-
ing these laws into connection with the case of Miriam -- Deut
24:8-9! We summarize Lev 13:9-17. When someone is leprous
(sr^ct, vs. 9, cf. Num 12:10) he is brought to the priest; if
the priest finds raw ("living") flesh (bśr ḥy), he pronounces
the leper unclean, and does not "shut him up" (sgr, vs. 11, cf.
Num 12:14-15), If, however, the leprosy covers his whole body,
and it has all turned white, the priest pronounces the leper
clean (vss. 12-13, 16-17). In our passage, therefore, Miriam's
whiteness, and her being "shut up", point not to active but to
"burnt out" leprosy. Her leprous flesh is dead flesh, the
disease has consumed it (cf. "dead" and "consumed" in Aaron's
simile in vs. 12!) She has been miraculously transformed
into a post-leprous condition; not rendered unclean, but
marked. Aaron's appeal to Moses, and Moses' to Yahweh, is for
her miraculous restoration to the pre-leprous condition (it is
tempting to make a connection between this passage and Ex 4:6-
7, in which Moses himself is afflicted with white leprosy and
then restored). The obscure vs. 14 seems to suggest that
Yahweh refused this appeal, but nonetheless reduced the punishment to a minimum. Again, the levitical laws may provide insight. Miriam's exclusion from the camp in vss. 14-15, as the
use of sgr shows, is for the period necessary to verify her
cleanness. Leviticus does not state that this was the same
for alleged burnt-out leprosy as for suspected beginning leprosy, but there is no reason to doubt it, and it consisted
(Lev 13:4-6) of three examinations at intervals of a week.
What Yahweh perhaps does, then, is to reduce Miram's trial
period from two weeks to one.

1.12   Analysis of narrative programs

1.120   In what follows, a "program" is the sequence of events,
carried out or merely conceptualized, whereby an actor in the
narrative seeks to bring about some result. Programs can be
presented by use of Greimas's actantial scheme of six actants
introduced in the previous chapter (I.3.11):

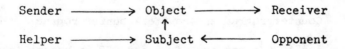

We hypothesize the following <u>main</u> <u>program</u> (MP) for our whole
narrative:

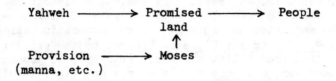

Activities directed against this main program (rebellions) will
be called counterprograms (CP), and activities of Yahweh to turn
these back, counter-counterprograms (CCP).

1.121   The main program

         The main program has left its traces throughout our
narrative. The itineraries (11:35; 12:16) are related to it
directly. In SB, the people's desire for meat conceals a desire to return to Egypt, counter to MP (and we note the frequent identification of the rabble with the "mixed multitude"
of Ex 12:38 -- a link with Egypt). In SC, Moses refers (11:12)
to his task of carrying the people to the promised land, and it
is possible that in vs. 15 he hints at Yahweh's inability or
unwillingness to carry out MP (cf. the tiqqūn sōph^{e}rîm, i.e.
one of the early alterations of the text to avoid offense; the
text may originally have read "your evil", in the sense of
Yahweh's evil intention, rather than "my evil", in the sense
of Moses' misfortune). One should perhaps take note here also
of the presence of Joshua (vs. 28), the one who will in fact
lead the people into Canaan. Most clearly of all, in SD, the
effect of Miriam's exclusion from the camp (and therefore of
her rebellion) is the delay in the people's march (12:15).
Under MP movement is positive and delay negative. Only in SA,
therefore, is there no overt reference to MP; but there are good
arguments in favor of following the tradition (e.g. Calvin:
15; Rashi: 52b) that the people are complaining in 11:1 about
the march itself. The march has just resumed, after Sinai, and
the immediately preceding verses (10:33-36) are directly on
this theme. SA, moreover, has no itinerary, that is, no notice
of the progress of the march.

1.122   Counterprogram and counter-counterprogram

1.1221   In SA, the pattern of CP and CCP is uncomplicated --

when the rebellion comes to Yahweh's attention he acts directly
to stop it; the agents of the CP are brought in line with the
CCP, and equilibrium restored. Matters are much more developed,
and also more complicated, in the other stories. The first dis-
tinctive feature of SB, SC, SD is that their CPs all seek diversification of what is unified in MP. In SB this diversification is twofold; the people not only seek to diversify the diet
of manna (11:5-6), but are also willing to diversify their own
oneness as the people of God by being joined to the rabble.
In both SC and SD, diversification of Israel's leadership is
sought, first by Moses himself, then by Miriam and Aaron. In
summary, these CPs challenge the integrity in turn of the three
underlined actants of our actantial schema (see 1.120):

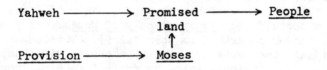

In each case, the ultimate aim of Yahweh's CCP is the restoration of unity.

1.1222   We have discovered two instances of instigation as
part of the CPs, in SB and in SD. The rabble aims not merely
to get meat, but to have the people join them in this aim;
likewise Miriam aims not merely to share the leadership, but
to have Aaron join her in this aim. In each case punishment
falls not on the seduced party (though the text makes reference to the possibility of it!), but only on the seducers.

1.1223   A particularly significant part of the analysis is
Yahweh's relationship to the CPs, the acts of rebellion. Instead of moving directly to a CCP, he cooperates with the CP,
makes himself, in fact, the operating subject of it; only
later does the real CCP emerge. In SB, he provides the meat
which the people desire. In SC, he provides the assistants
whom Moses desires. And even in SD, he joins Miriam and Aaron
to Moses, the leader, at the tent of meeting, the locus of
leadership (12:4), before separating them from both Moses and
the tent (vs. 5) /7/. This deception introduces into the narrative the issue of knowledge vs. ignorance -- rebels do not
know what Yahweh is really doing (see 2.12).

1.2   Syntagmatic narrative analysis

1.21   SC and SD. The most obvious superficial connection
between different stories in Num 11-12 is between SC and SD --
the themes of Moses' leadership and of prophecy, and the location at the tent of meeting. But the connection is deeper, for
the two stories are dovetailed together. The two CPs are
identical, the sharing of Moses' leadership with others, though
their subjects are different, Moses himself in SC, Miriam and
Aaron in SD. At the level of this common CP, SD resolves what
SC leaves unresolved. At the end of SC, Eldad and Medad are
left prophesying, by means of a spirit derived not from Moses,
but from Yahweh directly, and this means some diminution of
Moses' unique honor. In SD, two other "prophets", Miriam and
Aaron, challenge that uniqueness on the basis of Yahweh's having spoken through them independently of Moses. They are re-
buked and Yahweh departs from them (12:9). This departure
surely signals the departure of the prophetic gift they have
enjoyed (in what follows, Aaron is content to act through
Moses, vs. 11!). In fact, there are two points being made; a
static one, prophecy is inferior to Moses' leadership (2.123),
and a dynamic one, in that even prophecy disappears in the
course of the "combined" narrative.

1.22   SB and SC + SD

1.221   These sections, with their contrasted themes (provision of food, leadership-prophecy) have been intertwined,
with three sequences each. Furthermore, if we ignore 1:10, 13,
which link SB with SC, and lay out the sequences,

SB:	11:4-9	11:18-24a	11:31-34
SC + SD:	11:11-12, 14-17	11:24b-30	ch. 12

we discover that the three stages, in each case, come close to
coinciding with the steps CP, Yahweh's cooperation with CP, CCP,
which we analyzed in 1.122.

1.222   SB and SC have been "logically" connected at the surface level; loosely, it must be admitted, for it is not obvious
how the 70 elders, even if they assumed a full share of Moses'
responsibility, could be of assistance in finding meat for the
people. Two of the joins between sequences of SB and SC merit
attention. Curious, but of doubtful significance, is the

juxtaposition of two meanings of rwḥ, "spirit (of prophecy)"
and "wind", in 11:26-29 and vs. 31; Yahweh uses his rwḥ in each
instance to cooperate with a CP /8/. More obviously significant is the setting of the SB sequence 11:18-24a. Moses hears
and communicates to the people Yahweh's "words" (vs. 24a), and
is himself told to expect verification of Yahweh's "word" (vs.
23). Forming an inclusio around this section from SB are the
statements in SC (vss. 17 and 25) that Yahweh "speaks" with
Moses alone before distributing his spirit to the elders.
(The noun or the verb dbr are used in all cases). We have
argued that this feature of SC functions to undermine Moses'
CP there (see 1.1132), and the enclosed SB sequence strength-
ens this function (Yahweh continues to operate "normally",
through Moses alone, even in the context of sharing his
leadership with others.) We have argued earlier (1.1122)
that even SB, a story about the murmuring of the people, throws
its message heavily onto the character Moses. When we add to
this that SB provides the occasion for SC, and functions to
confirm the movement of SC, the overwhelming conclusion is that
leadership/prophecy is the most fundamental issue of Num 11-12.

1.23   The character Moses and the unity of the section

1.231   What has just been said confirms the central importance of Moses, who, indeed, alone appears in all four stories.
We must now pay attention to the roles that he plays. At the
beginning (SA) he only passes on to Yahweh appeals that he has
received. He institutes no programs, nor is any question
raised about his leadership position. But the same may be
said about the latter part of SD. Culley (101-10) has demonstrated a close similarity between SA and SD, and in fact we
may carry his parallels a little further than he does:

		SA	SD
(i)	Offense (complaint)	11:1	12:1-2
	Yahweh's overhearing of this	1	2
(ii)	Punishment by Yahweh	1	9-10
	Kindling of his anger	1	9
	Physical effects	1	10
(iii)	Appeal to Moses	2	11-12
(iv)	Appeal by Moses to Yahweh	2	13
(v)	Limitation of the punishment	2	14-15
	(but the physical effects remain)		

Our immediate point is the parallel mediary roles Moses plays
in the two instances. But the two ways in which he appears
in SD (passive object of a discussion about leadership, active
mediator) make it clear that SD fulfils two separate functions,
to "complete" SC (see 1.21), and to parallel SA. If we call
SD in these two aspects respectively SDa and SDb, we find that
the two functions are fulfilled to a large extent by different
parts of SD, roughly as follows:

$$SDa \ = \ 12:1^*, \ 2-9$$

$$SDb \ = \ 12:1-2, \ 9-15$$

We are here positing different functions, not (as in the case
of SB and SC) separate stories welded together /10/.

1.232   Hence, and particularly in relation to the roles
played by Moses, we may posit the following syntagmatic scheme
in Num 11-12:

$$
\begin{array}{c}
(\quad \ SB \quad \ ) \\
SA \ -- \ (\qquad\qquad) \ -- \ SDb \\
(\ SC \ + \ SDa \ )
\end{array}
$$

with parallelism between beginning and end, and intertwining
parallelism in the middle (see 1.221). In SA, Moses fulfils an
unquestioned mediary role, and he returns to it in SDb. But
in SC, he begins to take responsibility for his position, to
question it, and thereby to institute a program which is counter to Yahweh's main program. In SDa, however, he takes no
position on the program of Miriam and Aaron threatening his
leadership, leaving the matter entirely to Yahweh (12:3). A
pattern emerges in which Moses as passive channel is the norm,
from which he departs, and which departure must be "overcom-
pensated" before normalcy can be restored:

But what part does SB have to play in this? Several things
may be said. Within SB, we discover Moses attempting to take

responsibility for the action (11:13, 21-22), though at length
he is willing to be simply the channel for Yahweh's word (vs.
24a). We have suggested that the provision of immense quan-
tities of quail is a demonstration primarily for _him_ (vs. 23,
see 1.1122). But he is oddly absent from its fulfilment in
vss. 31-34, the last part of SB, which marks the hinge between
Moses' still ambiguous position at the end of SC and his unquestioned uniqueness in SDa. It seems possible, refining the
scheme just laid out for SA-SC-SD, to say that each change in
Moses' status is anticipated by his role in SB:

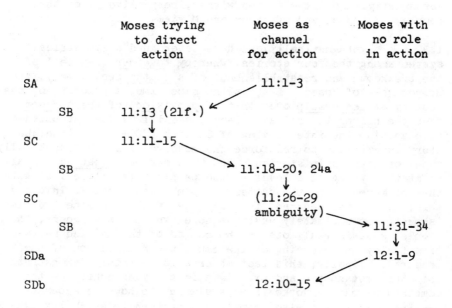

	Moses trying to direct action	Moses as channel for action	Moses with no role in action
SA		11:1-3	
SB	11:13 (21f.)		
SC	11:11-15		
SB		11:18-20, 24a	
SC		(11:26-29 ambiguity)	
SB			11:31-34
SDa			12:1-9
SDb		12:10-15	

1.3   Summary of the narrative analysis

1.31   Paradigmatically, we have determined a hierarchy of
narrative programs linking the four stories in Num 11-12; a
main program which is sometimes implicit, but which comes to
the surface at several points, and counterprograms and counter-
counterprograms displaying a number of recurrent features.
Most important, the CPs aim at the _diversification_ of what in
the MP is a _unity_, so that the CCPs seek to restore the unity.
In SA, the relations between MP, CP, and CCP are uncomplicated.
But in the other stories there are two main complicating fac-
tors. In SB and SD, firstly, we discovered the phenomenon of

instigation, in which the author of the CP tried, with initial
success, to secure the collaboration of a second party. In
these cases, the story includes the final separation of seducer from seduced, and the punishment of the seducer only --
the rabble and Miriam (who, though later reintegrated, was
marked) -- whereas the seduced are only threatened with a
punishment (11:19-20; 12:11) which does not occur. Secondly,
in SB, SC, and SD we found the phenomenon of Yahweh's apparent
cooperation with the CP, before the final clarification and
carrying through of the CCP -- Yahweh, that is, made moves towards carrying out the stated wishes, respectively, of the
people, of Moses, and of Aaron and Miriam.

1.32   Syntagmatically, we have determined a symmetrical
system among the four stories, whereby together they tell of
the breakdown and reestablishment of a status quo, namely, the
proper role of Moses. But, at the same time, a priority of the
isotopy of leadership over that of provision (of the subject
over the helper in Greimas's terms, see 1.120) was established
by examining the interweaving of SB with (SC + SD) -- the quail
story functioning to reinforce the message of the hierarchically
superior leadership stories. But this suggests instigation also at the syntagmatic level -- the people's rebellion instigates
that of Moses. And the pattern of punishment again reinforces
this; Moses, the seduced, is threatened with a permanent diminishment, but ultimately sustains none, while his seducers, the
people, sustain real loss in the course of the unified narrative (delay, the burning of the camp, the humiliation of their
leaders). Finally, this last observation not only demonstrates
that the syntagmatic and paradigmatic analyses cohere -- the
combined narrative works in ways similar to how the separate
stories work -- but also completes a pattern in which instigation and Yahweh's cooperation always go together; it is with
instigated CPs that Yahweh at first "goes along" (the desire
for meat, the desire to give up leadership, and the desire to
usurp leadership, instigated respectively by the rabble, the
people, and Miriam). There is a structural connection between
these two superficially unrelated features.

2.   Semantic analysis

2.1   The major isotopies

2.10   The two isotopies most fruitful for gathering the

message of our text are, we believe, suggested already by the
foregoing narrative analysis. The first includes unity and diversity. The second, less obvious, has to do with the communication of knowledge, epistemology; it is suggested in the first
instance by the recurrence of instigation in the CPs, and of
Yahweh's cooperation with the CPs. Our initial hypothesis is
that those seduced are regarded as deceived, who must be un-
deceived, and that Yahweh's mode of action maximizes awareness.
Our first task is to draw together and analyze all the features
of the text capable of being subsumed under these isotopies.
In each case it will prove possible to relate the isotopy directly to our hypothesized main program.

2.11   The isotopy of hierarchical organization

2.111   We have seen (1.1221) how the CPs seek diversification of unified elements of MP (Yahweh's provision, Moses'
leadership, Israel's integrity). The opposition is one vs.
many. But, in the case of Israel's temptation to join with
the rabble, we might better express it as separate vs. mixed
(cf. Septuagint epimiktos for the "rabble" of 11:4, using, as
the Hebrew does not, the same word as in Ex 12:38, "mixed
multitude"; for evidence that MT implies the identity of the
two groups, see 4.5). The same is true of other cases of
instigation -- conjunctions are established which are perceived
as bad, and the CCPs achieve the necessary separations (between Miriam and Aaron, and between Israel and Moses). That
unity and separation are both on the positive side of this
isotopy is not paradoxical; what is conceived is a hierarchy
of unmixed entities. (We shall justify this assertion with
reference to the codes to be considered in 2.2).

2.112   A few further points will suggest the scope of this
isotopy. To it belong the concepts of purity and of bounda-
ries. Both appear together in SA, where Yahweh begins to burn
the camp inwards from its perimeter; and Miriam is likewise
purified ($^{\circ}kl$, 12:12), and must cross and recross the boundary
of the camp (the same boundary is significant in 11:31-34).
Purity implies oneness with Yahweh (the consecration of the
people in 11:18, as opposed to their alienation from him in
vs. 20); but proper separation from Yahweh is also demanded
(12:5-8)!

2.12   The isotopy of communication and knowledge

2.120   This isotopy has two separate levels; Yahweh's direct
action in providing <u>awareness</u> of the nature of MP (2.121-122),
and his action to restore the means of permanent <u>communication</u>
of awareness, the position of Moses (2.123).

2.121   In dealing with the complex epistemological signals
in our text, we find helpful Greimas's concept of <u>veridiction</u>
(e.g. 1973a: 165-66):

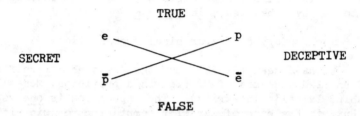

We retain, for convenience, the sigla e, that which <u>is</u> the case,
p, that which <u>appears to be</u> the case, and their negatives, $\bar{e}$
and $\bar{p}$ (derived from <u>être</u> and <u>paraître</u>). There are four states
of veridiction; if <u>truth</u> is the coincidence of appearance and
reality, and <u>falsity</u> the opposite, then what is but does not
appear to be is <u>secret</u>, and what is not but appears to be is
<u>deception</u>. If we apply this scheme to the reality/appearance
of blessing/curse in our text, then MP can be mapped onto it.

$$Egypt = \bar{e} + \bar{p} \text{ (false)}$$
$$Canaan = e + p \text{ (true)}$$
$$Desert = e + \bar{p} \text{ (secret)}$$

In Egypt, there is no blessing, nor the appearance of it (this
is the <u>text's</u> understanding, not that of the people's reminis-
cing in <u>11:5!</u>). In Canaan, there will be both blessing and
the appearance of it. The desert march represents true blessing, but not yet the appearance of it. In other words, the
transformation ($\bar{e} \longrightarrow e$) took place in the Exodus, but the
transformation ($\bar{p} \longrightarrow p$) will not occur until the entry into
the land. The important ideas of <u>interim</u> and <u>delay</u> are thus
introduced. Yahweh's aim in the desert is to <u>maintain belief</u>
in the reality of ($\bar{e} \longrightarrow e$) while ($\bar{p} \longrightarrow p$) is delayed. The

CPs (clearly in the case of the food) can be interpreted as demands for a <u>premature</u> ($\bar{p} \longrightarrow p$). Those led astray do not realize that such a premature transformation would effect another one, ($e \longrightarrow \bar{e}$), resulting in <u>deceptive</u> blessing:

$$CP \longrightarrow \bar{e} + p \text{ (deceptive)}$$

Such a program reverses the true conceptions of Egypt and Canaan (cf. now 11:5!), and can only lead, when appearance catches up with reality ($p \longrightarrow \bar{p}$), to a "return to Egypt". It is clear that delay is integral to Yahweh's intentions; ($\bar{p} \longrightarrow p$) must occur when he chooses if it is not to entail ($e \longrightarrow \bar{e}$) (since true blessing, in other words, comes from being in line with Yahweh's will). But, to maintain belief in the reality of the Exodus transformation ($\bar{e} \longrightarrow e$), Yahweh demonstrates <u>proleptically</u> his power to effectuate ($\bar{p} \longrightarrow p$), by his <u>cooperating</u> with the CPs, but never to the point of carrying them through. This necessitates a kind of counter-deceit (what <u>is</u> Yahweh's will vs. what <u>appears</u> <u>to</u> <u>be</u>). The situation can be presented as follows:

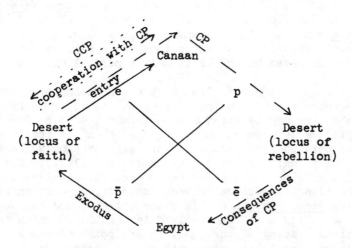

Unbroken line = MP (achieved and awaited)
Broken line = CPs (and their consequence)
Dotted line = Yahweh's counteraction (CCPs,
                but including cooperation with CPs)

One location, the desert, has here two conceptually separable
aspects. This coincides, of course, with the whole "double
tradition" of the desert in the Old Testament -- a place of ex-
emplary faith in, or of unexampled rebellion against, Yahweh
(Coats: passim).

2.122   The above typology can be fleshed out from the text,
and a number of details related to it.

2.1221   The CPs and ignorance. In SA, SB, SD, the complaints
embodying the CPs are undirected; that Yahweh "overhears",
rather than being the direct addressee, is clearest in 12:2, but
seems to be the case also in 11:1, 18. The complainants, in
other words, have no clear idea of who is to be the acting
subject of their CPs. Moses' complaint in SC differs in being
directed to Yahweh, but he still makes no actual request. A
number of details in his speech belong to our epistemological
isotopy; Moses does not know where "favor in Yahweh's eyes"
is to be found (cf. /4/), and fails to assess correctly the
people's desire for meat, his own responsibility, or the power
of Yahweh (1.1123). Even in vs. 29 he still seeks the democratization of his office! The CPs are born in ignorance (cf.
Aaron's "acting foolishly" in 12:11), in a breakdown of communication with Yahweh. If Yahweh cooperates with them, it is
on his own initiative, not in response to a request communi-
cated to him. Even Moses' CP is only a partial exception.

2.1222   Cooperation with CPs and the maximizing of awareness.
Yahweh's cooperation with the CP is complicated in SB by the
notion that the quails are for a punishment, a fact of which
the people are aware even as they gather them. A traditional
theme has perhaps here become semantically overloaded, and we
are not fully confident of our explanation (1.1122). But SB
is particularly productive for our present discussion in two
ways; the clear connection between Yahweh's cooperation with
CP and the demonstration of his power (11:23); and the deceptive ($\longrightarrow$ false) blessing involved in the CP, in which the
hypothetical eating of the quail to the point of nausea
(where it will no longer appear to be a blessing) may be interpreted as the final transformation ($p \longrightarrow \bar{p}$), closing the
circle in our diagram. In SC, these aspects are weakened, but
still present, in that Yahweh can share Moses' spirit with the
70, and Moses does suffer diminishment. In SD, the cooperation with CP is not stressed. Finally, in SB and SC there may

be narrative "clues" that the cooperation with CP is really a
part of the CCP -- the people's consecrating themselves,
attaching themselves to Yahweh even as they rebel (11:18); and
Yahweh's speaking to Moses alone even as his uniqueness is
threatened (neither element makes any obvious contribution to
the narrative).

2.1223   The CCPs and awareness. In the establishment of the
CCPs and the restoration of the status quo, the most obvious
epistemological element is the speech of Yahweh in 12:6-8, full
of information that the rebels have overlooked (see 2.123).
But there are other signals that the CCPs have confounded ignorance and restored communication; Aaron's confession (12:11);
the people's "completing" of their separation from the rabble
by burying them (11:34); and perhaps the giving of the place-
names, especially in 11:3, where the naming implies the correct interpretation of the event as divine punishment!

2.123   Communication and the figure of Moses. That our text
is not merely about communication of some content, but is also
about communication as such, is demonstrated above all in the
centrality of the issue of prophecy. In SC, the potential
leadership of the elders is reduced to prophecy, and in SD,
conversely, prophecy is no qualification for a leadership like
Moses'. The contrast between the two is brought out in 12:6-8,
the section most overtly devoted to epistemology. The main
point in the comparison is that, while prophecy is concerned
only with communication from Yahweh to Israel, Moses exercises
a two-way mediation between Yahweh and Israel. This is clear
from the definition of a prophet (vs. 6), and also in the
"mouth to mouth" of vs. 8 -- Moses talks back! It is further
suggested in "entrusted with all my house" (vs. 7), for, if
this at one level refers to Moses' special connection with the
tent of meeting, at a more important level it refers to his
responsibility for "the house of Israel" (Gray, 1903: 125). Not
merely, however, is Moses' mediary role a two-way one; even in
receiving communications from Yahweh he is superior to the
prophets. Communication in either direction, as we shall show,
is properly through him, and other communication is irregular
and/or ineffectual. In the terms of the first isotopy, there
is a unified and organized system of communication.

2.1231   First, communication from Yahweh to Israel. In 12:
6-8, once again, both Moses and the prophets both see and hear

Yahweh, but (i) Moses' hearing is better than the prophets'
("mouth to mouth" and "clearly" vs. "in a dream" and "in
dark speech"), and (ii) Moses' seeing is better than the prophets' ("sees the form of Yahweh" vs. "in a vision"). Even more
important is the contrast between communication mediated by
Moses, and that which is not. The prophecy of the 70 elders
is mediated (they partake of Moses' spirit), and this is signalled by Yahweh's speaking to Moses alone in their presence
(11:25). But the prophecy of Eldad and Medad is not mediated
by Moses, and such unmediated prophecy is claimed also by
Miriam and Aaron. Its flourishing is part of the CPs, and
the aim of the text is to lay it to rest (cf. our argumenta-
tion in 1.21); Yahweh speaks directly to Miriam and Aaron only
for the purpose of ending such irregularity, and its end is in
fact signalled again by Yahweh's speaking to Moses alone (12:14).

2.1232   Second, communication ...m Israel to Yahweh. Yahweh
as we have seen, is able to hear directly the complaints of the
rebels (2.1221), but they move him only to wrath and counteraction. His gracious response (stopping, or reducing the
effects of, his wrath) is only to communications made, at the
beginning and end of our text, through Moses (11:2; 12:11-14).

2.13   The intersection of the major isotopies

          The plane on which the two major isotopies, of hier-
archical organization and of communication and knowledge, coincide, is the centre of the text. The threat to Moses' position
of leadership does not attack MP merely in one detail; it
threatens the entire basis of MP, the established mode of communication between Yahweh and Israel. So Moses must not merely
be restored, he must be seen, by all parties, to be restored,
and the significance of his restoration understood.

2.2   The coding of the message of Num 11-12

2.20   The major isotopies which we have posited are of great
generality and abstraction. Only for the purpose of showing
their presence and broad shape have we related them to the details of our text, and this in a way which has paid little
attention to the semantic organization of the details themselves. The final part of our analysis is to display the codes,
natural or cultural systems, found in our text, and how the
major isotopies have been "transcribed" into them. The order

in which we introduce them is a matter of tactics; however we
do it, there will be details of one code whose full significance will not be clear until another code is introduced. At
the end (2.3) we shall summarize and organize these intercodal
connections, and frequent reference to this summary will facilitate the reading of the following paragraphs.

2.21 Geographical and temporal codes

We have sufficiently related the geographical code,
whose terms are Egypt, desert, Canaan, to the isotopy of knowledge (2.121). There is little explicit characterization of
these places in the text; suffice it to say here that the
desert is a place of _purification_ in the larger context (cf.
the "burning" desert with purification by fire). But another
code, the temporal (i.e. the system of time-references in the
text) can, we suggest, be subsumed under the geographical. The
point of all the time-references seems to be the _delay_ of the
march. CPs involve delay, and in this way strike directly at
the main program. This is clearest in the case of Miriam's
exclusion, but dealing with the quails also takes a stated
length of time (11:32), and perhaps it is no small part of
Yahweh's grace in keeping the people from meat that a month's
delay is thus avoided! The manna, on the contrary, falling by
night and gathered in the morning, does not delay the march.

2.22 Political-hierarchical code

2.221   Externally, Israel must be _one_, free from the admixture of foreigners (2.111). But internally, Israel is _many_
(the collective ᶜm, "people", provides very well for this
duality), and internal separations are established. That of
Moses is the most important. On his separation from other
potential leaders enough has been said; but his relation to
Israel as such needs further discussion. We have argued that
the people instigate Moses' rebellion (1.32), threatening an
improper conjunction between leader and led (a democratization,
we may say, which is just what Moses proposes to Yahweh in
11:29!). We therefore expect some textual signals of Moses'
separation from the people, and there appear to be at least
two. In 11:12, Moses _denies_ _kinship_ with Israel. This by
itself is hardly convincing, but it receives strong confirmation from the strange 12:1. The conjunction with foreigners
prohibited to Israel (a prohibition confirmed in the most

graphic way, by their burying of the rabble, <u>immediately</u> before
this verse!), is <u>permitted</u> to Moses (despite Aaron's and
Miriam's protest!). The other major separation achieved in the
text is between Miriam and Aaron which, at least at a first
level, is between female and male (for another aspect of this
separation, cf. 2.223). (The female Miriam instigates the male
Aaron to sin, putting herself thereby on the side of the foreign
rabble; women [e.g. Gen 3] and foreigners [e.g. Deut 7:4] are
great seducers, and the "foreign woman" the greatest of all
[Prov 2:16, etc.]!)

2.222   The hierarchy established by our text is as follows:

        Moses (raised above all others)
        Aaron (seduced, not punished, strongly
            repentant)
        People (both seduced and seducing,
            lightly punished, weakly repentant)
        Miriam (seducing, heavily punished, not
            repentant; restored but marked)
        Rabble (seducing, killed)   /11/

We cannot refrain here from a comment on the place-name Hazeroth
(<u>sc</u>. <u>onomastic</u> code) with which our text ends (12:16), and which
is provided with no etymology. Attempts to provide one have not
been welcomed (Noth, 1972: 224, with reference to Gressmann; but
cf. Eerdmans: 142). But the name means "enclosures", and is
identical to the term applied to the courts of the Temple. While
it may be fanciful to point to the parallel between our hierarchy
of people and the temple of Herod (holy of holies, courts of
Israel, women, and gentiles), we feel confident that the name
Hazeroth is a semantic marker for "separation" and belongs to
the first major isotopy.

2.223   With this hierarchy we may perhaps connect an obscurity
in the rebellion of Miriam and Aaron. Both claim that Yahweh
has established them as prophets (12:2). The larger narrative
supports Miriam's claim (Ex 15:20), but not Aaron's. Aaron is
proto-typically the <u>priest</u>, representing communication <u>from</u>
Israel <u>to</u> Yahweh. Therefore the rebellion appears to imply the
breakdown of the proper separation between, and hierarchization
of, offices. Another point from the larger narrative is curious,
and perhaps significant. Aaron's only other connection with

prophecy is when, in Ex 7:1, he is called <u>Moses'</u> prophet (spokes-
man before Pharaoh); in the light of this, Num 12 reads like a
reprise of the separation made in SC between prophecy derived
and not derived from Moses.

2.224   One significant figure has not yet been mentioned.
Joshua appears only at the tent of meeting (11:28, cf. Ex 33:11
and below, 2.2313), and his only contribution to the story is
to affirm Moses' sole leadership; he supports, as we have argued, Yahweh's MP against Moses' CP! There is an obvious link
with the <u>geographical</u> code: Joshua is cognate with Canaan
(into which he will eventually lead the people), that is, with
the true blessing; Moses is cognate with the desert (where he
will die), that is, with the ambiguous blessing, poised between
faith and rebellion (2.121). It was in the desert that Moses
met Yahweh (Ex 3, etc.) and, if, as seems likely, the text intends the identification of his Cushite wife with Zipporah
(Ex 2:21; 18:2) /12/, then Num 12:1 too recalls Moses' link
with the desert. We may perhaps go further, and see an opposi-
tion <u>older</u> <u>generation</u>/<u>younger</u> <u>generation</u> between Moses and
Joshua (Joshua'a collaborator in 11:27 is a n^{c}r,"young man");
it is the younger generation which will inherit Canaan with
Joshua, while the older will perish with Moses (14:28-35).

2.225   The "residue" (see O.3) from our analysis is, it must
be admitted, particularly great for the isotopy of <u>kinship</u> and
<u>sexual</u> relationships. We are unable, at this stage in the an-
alysis, to deal with the figurative use of this isotopy in
11:12; 12:12, 14. All deal with parent and child, suggesting
the older/younger generation opposition just discussed; and
12:14, the shaming of a daughter by her father, suggests also
the opposition male/female. But we cannot say more. Nothing
at all is made in our section of the kinship between Moses,
Aaron, and Miriam; indeed the very fact of it must be inferred
from the larger context. But it is no doubt part of the message of Num 12 that kinship does not imply sharing Moses'
leadership (Calvin: 41 latches onto nepotism, with its potential for causing disaffection, as the major issue in ch. 12!).

2.23   The topographical codes

2.230   The geographical code of the MP is, of course, a
special case of topographic coding. There are two other such
codes discernible in our text, so that the topographical coding
forms a very complex, but also very illuminating, system.

2.231   Tent-camp-outside the camp

2.2311   These terms are related in pairs, tent/camp and
inside/outside the camp, and SD is the only story to include
all three locations. Yet we believe they are to be understood
as forming one system. Their relationships may be approached
initially via topographical vocabulary /13/:

> (i) Sbyb(w)t, "around" appears in two places:
>   11:31-32, outside the camp.
>   11:24, near the tent, but at a remove from it.
> (ii) The verb ys᾽, "go/come out" is used as follows:
>   11:24, from the tent (presumably this is the
>   location of Moses' talk with Yahweh) to
>   the camp.
>   11:26; 12:4, from camp to tent.
>   12:5 (apparently) away from the tent.
> (iii) The verb ᾽sp ("to gather", nifal "to return") is
>   used in the following cases:
>   11:16, 24, from camp to tent.
>   11:30, nifal, from tent to camp.
>   11:32, towards the camp from outside (?)
>   12:14-15, nifal, from outside to inside the camp.

The last two verbs tend to suggest respectively centrifugal and
centripetal movement, and this fits those cases where the movement is between the outside and the inside of the camp. But
in the movement between tent and camp there is ambiguity, which
is probably to be explained from a conflict between tradition
and redaction. As is well known, our section has strong traditional links with Ex 33:7-11, where the tent of meeting is
clearly stated to be "outside the camp" (vs. 7, the same words
as in Num 12:14-15), so that one "goes out" to it from the
camp. But the present narrative of Num 11-12 cannot regard the
tent as being outside the camp, since it follows the long P
section which locates the tent in the middle of the camp (e.g.
Num 2:2). This creates no particular difficulty, since the
tent inside the camp did not begin to be built until Ex 36.
The insistence of pre-critical commentators (Keil and Delitzsch:
71) that the tent of Num 11-12 was in the middle of the camp
must, regardless of the history of tradition, coincide with
the assumption of the pentateuchal narrative we now have. We
must think, therefore, of a system of concentric spaces.

2.2312   Outside/inside the camp. The important relationship
between this boundary and <u>purification</u>, in SA and SD, has been
already noted (2.112). But the burning of the boundary in SA
may be paralleled in SB. The word used for "rabble", ᵓspsp,
is from the root ᵓsp, "gather", which is so prevalent in Num
11-12, and suggests "gathered ones", the foreigners gathered
around Israel's boundary. And in SB, they are precisely the
cause of the people's crossing the boundary to gather the quail
(which fall <u>outside</u> the camp, 11:31-32; on this see further
2.2432). The rabble is cognate with "outside" (just as it is
cognate with Egypt, Ex 12:38):

$$\frac{\text{Rabble}}{\text{People}} = \frac{\text{Outside the camp}}{\text{Inside the camp}}$$

The destruction of the rabble is thus the purifying of the alien
edge of Israel.

2.2313   Camp/tent. The two-way system of communication (2.123)
has its locus at the tent of meeting, where Yahweh appears, and
where Moses and Joshua have privileged places (12:7, Ex 33:7-11).
The tent is the locus of "regular", the camp of "irregular",
leadership. In SC, Eldad and Medad remain in the camp. The
70, for their regular ordination, go to the tent and are there
associated with Moses. It is interesting that when they return
(11:30), Moses comes with them, a signal of the ambiguity in
which his leadership stands, and that he is still in the camp
when SD opens (Joshua does not move from the tent). In SD,
Miriam and Aaron accompany Moses to the tent, but they are immediately moved away from it, and Moses left alone there.
(Miriam is unique in our two chapters in occupying at different
times all three locations, tent, camp, outside the camp; she
undergoes a pattern of up- and downswings the reverse of that
which we discovered for Moses (1.232):

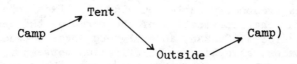

2.232   Vertical code.

        Yahweh descends (<u>yrd</u>) to the tent of meeting (11:17,

25; 12:5), and the same verb is used of the descent of the manna
(with the dew, 11:9). The quail likewise come out of the air,
but their origin is the sea (vs. 31), which is associated with
the subterranean, and there is another subterranean reference
in the burial of the rabble (vs. 34). There is thus a vertical
code of three terms, which we shall discuss more extensively in
relation to the alimentary code (2.2432).

2.233   The system of topographical coding

         The three codes may be summed up in the following
diagram:

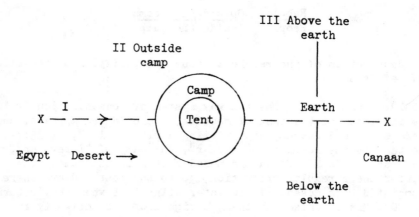

         I.   Geographical code
        II.   Tent-camp-outside the camp
       III.   Vertical code

I simply moves II and III laterally without altering them.
II and III intersect in various ways; Yahweh descends to the
tent, the manna on the camp (11:9), the quail outside it;
the rabble is presumably buried outside it. Each code has three
terms, and our characterization of the terms of the geographical
code (Egypt, desert, Canaan) as ambiguous space between two unambiguous spaces, as space for purification between impure and
pure, seems to hold for the other two codes (the alimentary code
will provide more evidence). Yahweh is associated with "Canaan"--
"above the earth" -- "tent", the impure rabble with "Egypt" --

"below the earth" -- "outside the camp". Between each of these pairs of terms the people pursues its ambiguous existence.

2.234   A sub-code: "vitality"

This system is confirmed by a code which we may call that of vitality, whose terms are death-sickness-health (life). Moses' death-wish (11:15) belongs to his CP, but there is no further development of it. Miriam's leprosy takes her "outside the camp", to which she may return only when her cleanness is established (1.1142). Most interesting is the mkh, "stroke" of 11:33. In the larger narrative this is to be understood as "sickness", and suggests the sickness associated specifically with Egypt (in Deut 28:59, 61 mkh is parallel to "sickness", which in vs. 60 is characteristic of Egypt; and 1 Sam 4:8, in a context stressing disease (5:6, etc.), uses mkh for the plagues of the Egyptians). This sickness proceeds explicitly to death and burial for the rabble, and implicitly back to health for the people (cf. 1.1121). Thus the terms of this code are related, to some extent, to those of each of the topographical codes.

2.24   Alimentary code

2.240   The treatment of foods in SB pulls together many elements of our discussion, and we shall proceed by relating this new code to the major isotopies and codes already presented.

2.241   Food and the isotopy of hierarchical organization

The people desire many foods, instead of the one ordained (11:5-6). This desire is instigated by the mixed rabble (vs. 4), who threaten the unity of the people. A propos this passage, Keil and Delitzsch (67) appositely contrast "the quiet enjoyment of what is clean and unmixed" with the desire for "a stimulating admixture of what is sharp and sour" (our emphasis).

2.242   Food and the isotopy of knowledge

Manna is Yahweh's secret food, congruent with the desert qua locus of faith (2.121). We note its coming by night (11:9), and especially the etymology of Ex 16:15, "What is it?" It meets the people's needs rather than their wants (faith in Yahweh's secret blessing) -- it is not given, in

this passage, in answer to any request /14/. Particularly
interesting is the opposition temporary/permanent. The manna
does not last from day to day. The meat comes in abundance,
a 30 days' supply, but it is presumably subject to decay
(which perhaps is part of the thought behind the people's becoming nauseated with it, 11:20) /15/. The appropriate opposition is renewable sparseness/ once-for-all plenty (again, faith/
deceit). And yet another opposition seems relevant. The
people who desire the meat in fact reminisce (11:5) about food
which includes meat in the form of fish, but also various
vegetables, including the melon type. A comment of Lévi-Strauss
(1973: 468) is interesting:

> . . . fish and water-melons are not only sym-
> metrical because they belong respectively to
> the animal and vegetable kingdoms: considered
> as dry-season foods, fish is food enclosed in
> water, and the water-melon (especially in the
> dry season) is water enclosed in a food.

This confirms what the text itself makes clear, that the opposition wet/dry is here in play. For the people, the manna signi-
fies the dryness of the desert -- "our strength is dried up"
(or, "our throat is dry", Noth, 1968: 86, commenting on vs. 6;
appositely Keil and Delitzsch: 66, "the manna, sc. which has no
juice . . . "). But the "editorial" of vss. 7-9 questions this
view, associating the manna with the dew, the transitory water
of the desert! The editorial makes clear that the people are
deceived in their assessment of the manna. Yahweh supplies the
wet from the dry, just as he waters the desert (and provides
"water from the rock", Ex 17:1-7; Num 20:1-13), but in a way
mysterious and beyond human control.

2.243   Food and the topographical codes

2.2431   The people desire the food of Egypt, rejecting the
manna which is specific to the desert (it ceases at the moment
of entry into Canaan, Jos 5:12). But the manna belongs to the
geographical code in an even more important way. It is on the
side of movement, as against delay (2.21), more clearly than
any other element in the text. Just as there must be no delay
in using it (cf. 2.242), so no delay is involved in gathering
it. It comes by night, is collected early, and the march continues. Rebellion means delay, and quite specifically so in
the gathering of the quails (11:32).

2.2432   While manna falls on the camp (vs. 9), the quails
fall outside it (vs. 31), so the people must cross the boundary to get it. The quails are thus associated with the impure. Consistent with this, but much fuller, are the connections between foods and the vertical code. The manna shares
with the dew and with Yahweh himself the characteristic that
it descends, has its origin above the earth. The foods the
people crave come from below the earth, plants by growing up
out of it, fish by being lifted from the sea. Moses (11:22)
"recommends" both fish and cattle, which move on the surface
of the earth. The food Yahweh finally sends descends, but
this rather parodies than imitates the manna, since the quails
originate from the sea! Food which descends represents the
blessing, food which ascends, the curse. The quails (like all
CPs, 2.121) represent the deceptive blessing, apparently from
above, but really from below!

2.244   The manna and Moses

         At every point in the analysis parallels have appeared
between these elements, and it is worthwhile to summarize and
extend these parallels. Both the manna and Moses represent the
unity of Yahweh's MP against the diversity of the CPs. Both
are congruent with the desert, and both will "cease" precisely
at the end of the desert period. Just as the manna is Yahweh's
secret, so the blessing on Israel through Moses is constantly
unrecognized (cf. frequently in the desert tradition; here, cf.
Miriam's and Aaron's failure to recognize Moses' role, but also
his "meekness", 12:3). Finally, just as the renewable sparseness (reliable) of the manna is contrasted with the once-for-all
plenty (deceitful) of the quails (2.242), so the "once-for-all
plenty" of the prophecy of the 70 -- their large number and the
insistence that they prophesied only once -- points up the
"renewable sparseness" of the leadership of Moses alone. At a
deep level of our text, the signs "Moses" and "manna" function
together.

2.3   The semantic configurations of Num 11-12

         We here summarize the congruities which we have dis-
covered between the major isotopies and codes, drawing upon
Greimas's concept of configurations (1973a: 169-71). All the
elements in one column tend to carry the same basic element of
meaning in our text. There is, of course, fluctuation and

uncertainty in such a system, but the sketching of it should be
of special importance for further work on other parts of the
Old Testament (see below, 4), by which work it will, of course,
need to be refined:

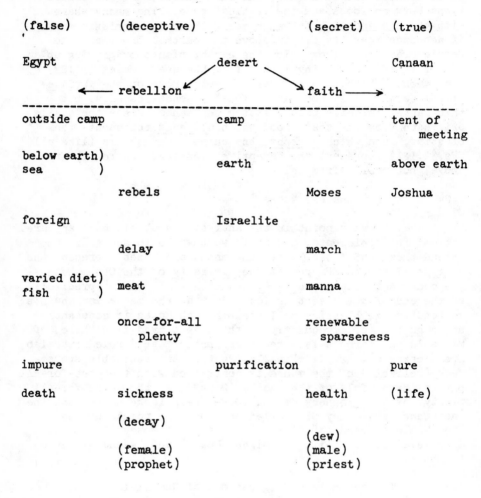

(false)	(deceptive)		(secret)	(true)
Egypt	desert			Canaan
	rebellion ←	desert →	faith →	

outside camp		camp	tent of meeting
below earth) sea)		earth	above earth
	rebels	Moses	Joshua
foreign		Israelite	
	delay		march
varied diet) fish)	meat		manna
	once-for-all plenty	renewable sparseness	
impure		purification	pure
death	sickness	health	(life)
	(decay)		
		(dew)	
	(female)	(male)	
	(prophet)	(priest)	

3.   The "myth" and its versions

3.0   We have made considerable use of pre- or non-critical
traditions of commentary, from Philo to Keil and Delitzsch, but
especially of rabbinic literature. There are two reasons for
this. First, such traditions are very sensitive to the movement

of narrative, and particularly to the points at which it becomes
problematic (superficial illogicalities, non sequiturs, etc.
We surmise that narratives become problematic at the points
where their meaning is "thickest" (cf. I.1.22) and it is this
thickness of meaning which pre-critical commentators often help
to locate (however we may feel about their interpretations).
Yet more importantly, we have consistently found that rabbinic
and other interpretations, though they seem far from a literal
reading of the text, often work strikingly within the isotopies
and codes which our analysis has determined in the text. Structural analysis may provide us with a new way of appreciating
such traditions of commentary, and of testing their coherence
with the results of critical methods. Methodologically, the
approach suggested here is close to that of Lévi-Strauss (1963:
217): " . . . we define the myth as consisting of all its
versions; or to put it otherwise, a myth remains the same as
long as it is felt as such". The following are a few examples;
for our limited purpose, we have made absolutely no attempt to
use the rabbinic literature critically.

3.1   The demand for meat cannot have been sincere, for the
people had plenty of cattle (Ex 12:38); the rabble simply sought
occasion for rebellion (Ginzberg: III, 245). What the people
were really upset about (reading in 11:10 "weeping over their
families") was the consanguineous marriages which they had con-
tracted before the giving of the law, and which they now would
have to give up (ibid., 246-247). The themes of kinship, and
of attachment/separation, are here pursued.

3.2   A persistent rabbinic tradition claims that the manna,
though one substance, would assume any desired taste (except,
in some versions, the tastes of the foods enumerated in 11:5
as characteristic of Egypt; Ginzberg: III, 245-246). The uni-
fying of the many in the one (with exclusion, however, of the
absolutely impure) is a fascinating development of our isotopy
of hierarchical organization.

3.3   Rabbinic sources hold that the prophecy of Eldad and
Medad was direct from Yahweh, and that it continued when that
of the 70 elders ceased. But they go on to inform us what it
was that the two prophesied, namely the death of Moses and
Joshua's leading the people into Canaan. Eldad and Medad were,
moreover, kin to Moses (and so to Miriam and Aaron), sharing
with them one parent (the sources differ as to which; Ginzberg:

III, 252-53). These traditions pursue the relationship between
kinship and leadership, and make plausible the use of the
Miriam-Aaron story to resolve the Eldad-Medad one. The prophecy about Moses and Joshua relates to the geographic code, and
particularly draws attention to 11:12 and 15, where Moses would
rather die than lead the people into the promised land. It
would be hard, in fact, to find a better example of legendary
elaboration finding its own way of following up the logic of
the story!

3.4   Elaborations of the trouble regarding Moses and his
Cushite wife (12:1) work in various ways with the idea of purity and the separation of Moses. The major rabbinic legend is
that Moses had withdrawn from cohabitation with Zipporah so as
to be always in readiness for Yahweh's commands; this commenda-
tion of sexual asceticism itself stresses Moses' uniqueness,
for it puts him above normal obligations (Gen 1:28; Ginzberg:
III, 256-58). Philo, we may add, interprets the Ethiopian
woman as "the nature that has been tried by fire and cannot be
changed" (Legum allegoriae, II 67 -- on purification by fire,
cf. above, 2.112!), while Origen develops the theme of Moses'
unique association with a gentile (131, cf. our 2.221).

4.   The extension of the analysis to other sections

4.0   Num 11-12 stands in a close relationship to other passages in the Pentateuch, and it is these passages which we envisage as the object of the next stage of analysis. Here we
do no more than identify them, and indicate their superficial
relationships with Num 11-12.

4.1   The traditions of rebellion in the desert. In the
long run, we shall need to pay attention to narrative sequence
in its largest dimensions, rather than to short sections only.
The scheme

          exodus - desert - Sinai - desert - conquest

should be fruitful. It relates to our geographical code; it
shows an alternation of complexes dominated by divine initiative (exodus, Sinai, conquest) with ones dominated by the initiative of human actors; and it encourages comparison between
the two desert-complexes, before and after Sinai. There are

many parallel stories in these two desert sections; the most
obvious difference is that the element of divine <u>punishment</u> is
absent from the first. The quail story in Num 11 has its
parallel in Ex 16, though the two show big differences (Ex 16
devotes most attention to the manna, and regards it and the
quail as <u>simultaneous</u> in origin). But Ex 16 and Num 11:4-35
share a curious characteristic. Each is the central and largest
pericope of a set of three (in the first case, the other two
sections are Ex 15:22-27 and 17:1-7) related to provision and/
or murmuring, and in each case the two outer sections belong
to the same story-type in Culley's classification (cf. above,
1.231, and for the Exodus material, Culley: 78-81, 83-87, 92-
96). Parallel analyses of Ex 15:22-17:7 and Num 11-12 should,
therefore, provide excellent insight into the relations between pre-and post-Sinai desert sections. (Among the thematic
links are purification [of the water in Ex 15:22-25], the
"diseases of Egypt" [vs. 26], the number 70 [vs. 27], and the
elders [17:5-6]).

4.2   We have made reference several times, in connection
with the tent of meeting, to Ex 33:7-11. We find there, in
addition to Yahweh's cloud theophany and Joshua's attendance on
Moses, the themes of Yahweh's speaking to Moses "face to face"
(cf. "mouth to mouth", Num 12:8), and the expression "at the
door of [a] tent", of which we have given no account in our
analysis, but which appears in Num 11:10 and 12:5. But the
material surrounding Ex 33:7-11 is also rich in thematic links
with our section: Moses' seeing Yahweh (33:20-23), Aaron's
rebellion (ch. 32), Moses' readiness for death (32:32), and
the reverse possibility -- Israel's death and Moses' fathering
of a new nation (32:10)!

4.3   Ex 18 draws together two of the important themes of
Num 11-12. .First, the sharing of Moses' leadership. As it
appears in Ex 18:13-27, this theme shows considerable differences from Num 11 -- it is on outside (Jethro's) advice, it
is carried through (with unquestioned good effects), and the
assistants are not called elders (though elders do appear in
the chapter, vs. 12, in connection with eating "before God",
cf. 4.4). But there are great similarities in phraseology:
"you are not able to perform it alone" (vs. 18, cf. Num 11:13),
"they will bear the burden with you" (vs. 22, cf. Num 11:17).
The second theme is Moses' marriage (Num 12:1 -- on the tradition that this wife was Zipporah, cf. 2.224). It is on his
<u>father-in-law's</u> initiative that Moses seeks assistance in the

administration, and Jethro has some intimate connection, despite his foreignness, with Yahweh (Ex 18:9-11). The separation,
at the end of this chapter, of Moses from his in-law, is of
significance for our section in the light of Num 10:29-32. Here,
Moses is still in company with a brother-in-law, whom he invites
to accompany Israel to Canaan (main program!). Hobab is reluc-
tant, Moses presses Israel's need of him, and the issue is left
unclear. In the light of those passages, Moses' ambiguous relationship to Israel must be analyzed much more deeply (2.221).

4.4   In Ex 24, 70 elders accompany Moses, Aaron (and two
other named individuals!), up Mt. Sinai, and the following
themes are to be noted: Moses' association with/dissociation
from the 70 (vss. 1, 2, 14), seeing God (vs. 11), eating and
drinking (ibid.). Joshua accompanies Moses, whose leadership,
in his absence, is taken over by Aaron and Hur (vs. 14) in
terms very like those of Ex 18. Yahweh is "like a devouring
fire" (vs. 17, cf. Num 11:1). And there is a final, very striking, verbal connection. In Ex 24:11 the elders are called
ᵓsylym (RSV, "chief men"), a word occurring nowhere else in the
Old Testament, but from the same root as in Num 11:17: "I will
take (ᵓsl) some of the spirit which is on you and put it on
them" (on which basis Gray, 1903: 116 says, "they may represent
variations from a common story"). Particularly fruitful is a
study of the rabbinic connections between the two groups of 70
elders in Ex 24 and Num 11 (e.g. the completely contrasting
views in Num R 15:21, 666-667 and ibid. 15:24, 668-671).

4.5   Our final connection is at once the most striking and
the hardest to assess. All the elements of the brief passage
Ex 12:37-39, the departure from Egypt, reappear in Num 11, in
our SB, but in such a disconnected way as to remind one only of
Lévi-Strauss's analyses of American myths, and of his concept
of "transformations" /16/!

Ex 12:37-39	Num 11 (SB)
Departure from Egypt	Nostalgia for Egypt (11:5)
600,000 Israelites	(vs. 21)
Mixed multitude	Rabble (vs. 4)
Flocks and herds	(vs. 22)
Poor food supply	The theme of SB
Grain food	Manna
Cakes (ᶜuggōt)	Cakes (ᶜuggōt) (vs. 8)

FOOTNOTES TO CHAPTER II

/1/   We do not here use syntagmatic and paradigmatic as
synonyms for "narrative" and "semantic" respectively, as other
authors commonly do. Our point here is that within our narrative (qua syntagm) there are sub-narratives in paradigmatic
relation to each other, though each is, of course, itself a
syntagm at another stage of analysis.

/2/   The remarkable relationship between SB and Ex 12:37-
39 (see 4.5) raises the possibility that the reference in vs.
21 to 600,000 Israelites deliberately excludes the rabble (who
in Ex 12 are specifically separate from the 600,000).

/3/   Rather than to the people (Keil and Delitzsch: 73).
Note the emphatic "you" (ᵓth) for "now" (ᶜth) in the Samaritan
version.

/4/   Calvin (22-23) aptly finds Moses to incriminate himself in vs. 11 (cf. vs. 15) -- there could be no more supreme
"favour in [Yahweh's] sight" than the leadership of Yahweh's
people.

/5/   Rejecting in vs. 25 the versional reading, accepted
for instance by Noth (1968: 89) "and they did not cease".

/6/   We follow Calvin (24-26; cf. Noth, 1972: 129) against
a long tradition (at least as old as Philo, De gigantibus 25)
that Moses' spirit, like a flame from which others are lit, lost
nothing by being shared. In Greimas's terminology, the trans-
action is not a "participative communication" (1973b: 32-34),
but rather the transfer of a substance.

/7/   This, at least, gives a consistent interpretation of
the odd double use of ysᵓ; vs. 4, "out from the camp to the
tent", vs. 5, "out from the tent".

/8/   Vs. 31 is one of the rare cases where rwḥ has mascu-
line gender.

/9/   Step (v) is certainly more complicated in SD, but we
have argued (against Culley: 105) that the physical effects
of Miriam's punishment do remain (see 1.1142).

/10/   No doubt the tradition did have separate stories; e.g.
Coats (262) offers the following analysis: "tradition of the
Cushite wife, 1, 10, 12-16; tradition of Moses' peculiar re-
lationship with Yahweh, 2 (3), 4-9, 11".

/11/   The elders do not figure here. They are scarcely
"actors", and the terms by which we have achieved our hierarchy
are not relevant to them.

/12/   The rabbinic literature normally makes the identification: Ginzberg (VI, 90).

/13/   Interesting also is the recurrent bqrb, "in the midst
of"; the rabble, Yahweh, and Moses are all said to be "in the
midst of" Israel (11:4, 20-21). It seems that these statements
of conjunction, in the light of our discussion, only signal the
need for the proper separations!

/14/   The same was probably true of one stage of the tradition in Ex 16: Coats (83-96).

/15/   Decay is an important theme of the desert traditions,
e.g. Deut 8:4. The tendency in folklore of supernatural gifts
to turn to dust, etc., is relevant to the manna; cf. Greimas
(1973b: 21-22).

/16/   We are preparing for publication an article on the
relationship between Judg 19-21 and 1 Sam 11, an even more
extraordinary example of two sections with many elements of
meaning in common, but superficially with no common pattern.

Chapter III
Ahab's Quest for Rain:
Text and Context in 1 Kings 17-18

> It is in this sense that a structure is "closed,"
> a notion perfectly compatible with the structure's
> being considered a substructure of a larger one;
> but in being treated as a substructure, a struc-
> ture does not lose its own boundaries; the larger
> structure does not "annex" the substructure; if
> anything, we have a confederation, so that the
> laws of the substructure are not altered but con-
> served and the intervening change is an enrich-
> ment rather than an impoverishment (Piaget: 14).

> He imitated Jeroboam the son of Nebat -- who not
> only sinned but made Israel sin -- so that he made
> Yahweh angry at their idolatry (1 Kg 16:26).

0.   Introduction

0.1   The problematic

This chapter will pursue a limited goal; to investigate, in the case of a single example, what we may call the "exchange of meaning" between a text and its context. Biblical
narrative exists mostly in very large units, and the analysis
of any sub-unit (by whatever method) must pay some attention to
the question: to what extent does the sub-unit derive its meaning from the context? But one can ask the converse question:
how does the sub-unit contribute to the meaning of the larger
narrative? To this universally familiar issue of "the whole
and the parts", structuralist theory has, we hope to show, something special to contribute. In Piaget's view, a complete,

self-regulating system may simultaneously be a part of a larger
system (13-16). To take the most obvious analogy, a sentence
must be built according to rules for well-formedness, while at
the same time it forms part of a paragraph or larger discourse.
Conversely, paragraphs are made of sub-units, sentences, which
satisfy rules of their own, as well as rules of paragraph-
building.

0.2   The text

0.21   The example chosen is the account of the drought in
1 Kg 17-18, and, within it, the combat on Mt. Carmel. Both of
these are, in a sense to be defined, "well-formed stories", but
one is a part of the other. It is our purpose to lay bare the
exchange of meaning which, at various levels, takes place between them. These two chapters have, of course, been the object
of extensive discussion, some of it very sensitive to the special
problems of narrative analysis. The best treatment, in our view,
is that of Smend, while Tromp offers a most interesting, and
more "literary", reading. Despite the differences in aim and
method, we and such scholars as these must often make decisions
on the same issues, such as the appropriate delineation of
stories. We shall refer to them in footnotes at points where
a comparison of views might be fruitful. The methodological
significance of the convergence or divergence between their
decisions and ours is, however, much too large an issue to be
taken up here (cf. the brief remarks in the Postscript 1.3.)

0.22   For sharpness of focus, the main part of our study
will be restricted in two ways. First, the drought story will
be dealt with only in skeleton form; we shall not consider the
account of Elijah and the widow of Zarephath (17:8-24), and
shall confine our treatment of Obadiah (18:3-16) to his formal
significance in the drought narrative. Second, we shall offer
only a narrative, and not a semantic, analysis (cf. II.0.3, and
the whole structure of Chapter II). In appendices (4.1-2) we
shall sketch the outlines of an analysis more complete in these
two respects. In a third appendix (4.3), we shall sketch the
continuation of the analysis in another direction -- the relation
of the entire drought story to its larger context.

0.3   The technical apparatus

0.30   We have made an effort to limit, and demystify, the

conceptual apparatus of this study. Structuralist procedures
and results may perhaps be expressible in normal English!
Narrative analysis has been developed to deal with two main
units, the story and the performance, and these will be the
units considered here.

0.31   V. Propp and the "story"

0.311   Propp, working on a large group of Russian folktales,
reduced them completely to 31 "functions", sequential items of
narrative, and found that, although no tale has them all, those
that do occur are always in the same order (Propp: 25-65).
These numerous functions are capable, retaining Propp's Roman
numerals, of a preliminary sub-grouping:

I-VIII   The "villainy" or "lack" (that disturbance of
           the status quo which sets the story in motion),
           and anything leading up to this.

IX-XIV   The finding of the hero, establishment of his
           willingness to undertake the quest (i.e. to re-
           store the status quo), and his qualification,
           whereby he receives necessary help (often a
           magic agent).

XV-XIX   The main combat, whereby the villain is de-
           feated or the lack overcome.

XX-XXXI   A variety of functions having to do with the
           hero's return, recognition, and exaltation,
           and the restoration of the status quo.

The arrangement will be of the greatest importance for our
discussion. To reduce Propp's scheme even more, the basic
movement in a story is from the "villainy" or "lack" (function VIII), to the "defeat" of the villain or "liquidation"
of the lack (functions XVIII, XIX). Propp goes on (79-80)
to enumerate seven typical dramatis personae of the tales;
of these the important ones for us are the villain and the
hero, whose roles are self-evident, and the pair donor, who
provides the hero with a magical agent, and helper, who (among
other things) gets him to the scene of combat. Propp's distinction between these two is confusing, and we shall use
"helper" for both.

0.312   The "well-formed story" is, of course, an intuitive
idea based on the recognition of coherence between Aristotle's
beginning, middle, and end. But Propp's preliminary work showed
it to be capable of illuminating analysis; and his results have
been transplanted with remarkable success from their original
Russian soil. A story will be considered "well-formed" if it
fits reasonably closely into Propp's scheme.

0.32   A. J. Greimas and the "performance"

0.321   Building on Propp's work, A. J. Greimas has developed
a scheme whereby any narrative happening, or even potential
happenings which fail to occur, can be described. The complete
unit is the <u>performance</u>. It can be described by the the now
well-known actantial model of six actants (I.3.11):

$$\text{Sender} \longrightarrow \text{Object} \longrightarrow \text{Receiver}$$
$$\uparrow$$
$$\text{Helper} \longrightarrow \text{Subject} \longleftarrow \text{Opponent}$$

0.322   The performance can be analyzed into three parts, and
these into six sub-sequences, "syntagms", as follows (cf. the
convenient presentation in Patte: 43-46):

    I.   Contract
         CS1   Establishment of volition
         CS2   Receiving of power/knowledge

   II.   Disjunction
         DS   Movement to location of the
               performance proper

  III.   Performance proper
         PS1   Confrontation
         PS2   Domination
         PS3   Attribution

         (CS = "contract syntagm", etc.)

A performance requires <u>first</u> that the subject acquire the <u>will</u>
or <u>volition</u> (CS1), and sufficient <u>power</u> and/or <u>knowledge</u> (CS2),
to carry it out (Greimas, 1970: 179). This occurs at the <u>con</u>-
tract stage. After the <u>disjunction</u>, the <u>performance</u> <u>proper</u>
consists of <u>confronting</u> and <u>dominating</u> the opponent, so that

the <u>attribution</u>, the transfer of the object to its intended receiver, can take place. In actual discourse, many of these
steps are implicit; but all are logically present, and failure
at any point will mean an <u>aborted</u>, non-actualized sequence.

0.323   The contract stage, the acquisition of the "modalities"
(cf. the "modal" verbs, "to want to", "to be able to", "to know
how to"), will be much the most important for our analysis.
We shall also occasionally use the idea of <u>domination</u> (PS2).
But what this technical terminology amounts to is, quite simply,
getting ready to do something, and then doing it!

0.33   The analogy between "story" and "performance"

        Though Greimas's scheme is of much greater generality
than Propp's, the two are parallel. Not only are Propp's
<u>dramatis personae</u> analogous to Greimas's actants /1/ but there
is close parallelism between Propp's functions and Greimas's
syntagms as organized by Patte:

<u>Propp</u>	<u>Greimas/Patte</u>
Finding the hero (IX-X)	CS1
Getting help (XII-XIV)	CS2
Transfer to location of object (XV)	DS
Combat (XVI)	PS1
Victory (XVIII)	PS2
Liquidation of lack (XIX)	PS3

A story, we may say, is a performance writ large, while every
intended action is a sort of quest.

1.   The drought

1.1   The delineation of the text

        We first hear of a drought in Ahab's time at 1 Kg 17:1,
and at 18:45 the drought is broken. The section 17:1-18:45,
therefore, moves from the establishment of a lack to its liquidation, which is the basic movement of Propp's scheme /2/. For
the present, this "story" is the object of our investigation.

1.2   The Ahab-quest story

1.21   We begin by "retelling" the story of the drought /3/:

> King Ahab received a visit from Elijah, who an-
> nounced that no rain would fall without his per-
> mission, and then disappeared. Ahab sent to every
> country to try to find Elijah, without success.
> When drought and famine were far advanced, Ahab
> organized a search for any vegetation remaining
> in his kingdom. He found not vegetation, but the
> whereabouts of Elijah. On confronting Elijah,
> Ahab accused him of causing the drought. But
> Elijah replied that Ahab was the real cause, on
> account of an offense that he and his family had
> committed. Elijah made Ahab undergo a test, and
> when he passed it, caused rain to fall. Ahab
> returned home.

In telling the foregoing story, we have remained very close to
1 Kg 17-18, indulging in minimal reconstruction by putting the
part of the story told by Obadiah (18:10) in its proper chronological place. The story in this form tells of a successful
quest undertaken by Ahab. The analysis proceeds by observing
how our text both encourages and undermines this retelling of
the story.

1.22   On the positive side, a Proppian analysis works well.
The villain, Elijah, steals rain (17:1). The hero, Ahab, sets
out in quest of rain, that is, of Elijah, and gets to the right
place by the agency of a helper (18:2b-16). Thus Propp's
scheme works strikingly well for functions VIII-XIV, the "villainy" and the qualification sequence. As a result of a "combat" with Elijah (18:17-20), Ahab gets the rain (18:41-45).
His return home after his success (18:45) also fits the Proppian pattern.

1.23   Yet our attempt to read the story thus is obviously in-
adequate and unconvincing, bombarded with difficulties from all
sides. Let us enumerate the major problems. First, immediately
after the "villainy" (which covers all of 17:1-5, since Elijah's
disappearance is an integral part of the problem) come sub-
sequences which are not directly a part of the movement of the
main story (vss. 6-7, and especially 8-24). That there should

be sub-stories is not in itself surprising; what is surprising
is that they should be about the villain rather than the hero.
Second, the initiative for the crucial meeting comes (humanly
speaking) from the villain, Elijah (18:2a). Ahab does indeed
take some initiative (vss. 3a, 5), but he has apparently given
up the search for Elijah, and the meeting is, from his standpoint, fortuitous. Again, one expects the initiative for combat to come from the hero /4/. Third, the sequence of the
helper, Obadiah (vss. 3-16), takes a form strikingly similar to
a complex tale discussed by Propp (133-34), in which twin heroes
take separate roads (cf. vs. 6) to diverse fortunes. Ahab is
here the one who goes off in the "wrong" direction, so that
this sequence yet again calls in question his capacity as hero.
Fourth, 18:17-20 does not at all answer to the expected combat;
but it is just at this point that a real combat occurs (vss.
21-40), in which Ahab is not involved! The final verses of the
story (41-45) are not entirely clear, but there is little to
be said about them /5/. Ahab "fulfils" his quest, but as no
more than an onlooker. He does whatever Elijah tells him to
do, and no more (vss. 41-42, 44-45); he returns home as a
parody of a hero, having the rain he set out for, but having
played no part in the obtaining of it. In summary we may say
that the story of Ahab's quest and Elijah's villainy has been
systematically dismantled even as it was being told!

1.3   The Ahab-villainy story

1.31   Our retelling of the story has been found to stand
in a dialectical, both positive and negative, relationship to
the text itself. The clue to this duality lies in 18:17-18.
These verses, in which the reader intuitively recognizes the
climax of the drought story, in fact upend the story told up
to this point, and create an implicit new one. In the new
story, Ahab is the villain, not the hero. He has "forsaken
the commandments of Yahweh and followed the Baalim", and for
this reason, it is implied, Yahweh has withheld the rain.

1.321   The new story involves other actors. Ahab's house-
hold is implicated in his crime. Jezebel is not named here,
but in other pieces of the new story with which the text has
provided us (vss. 4, 13, 19) she is deeply involved in the
villainy, having killed Yahweh's prophets and nurtured those
of Baal. But the importance of Jezebel is in relation to the
larger context of the drought story (cf. 4.3). More important

for present purposes is "Israel". The role of the people is
not an active one, but rather that of pure victim of Ahab's
villainy. He is the "troubler of Israel". "Troubler" means
"one who puts in cultic jeopardy" /6/, so that the people of
Israel are victims of Ahab's apostasy, not merely in lacking
rain, but also in having been led away from Yahweh.

1.322   The program (cf. II.1.120) of the new story is thus
revealed. The purpose of the drought has been to induce Ahab,
who has led the people astray, to lead them back to Yahweh; in
Greimas's scheme:

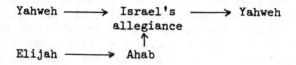

$$\text{Yahweh} \longrightarrow \text{Israel's} \longrightarrow \text{Yahweh}$$
$$\text{allegiance}$$
$$\uparrow$$
$$\text{Elijah} \longrightarrow \text{Ahab}$$

1.33   18:17-18 is for Ahab, as for the reader, the epistemological turning-point; here he learns what has been going on
all the time! This brings us to vss. 19-20, which form the join
between the enclosing story of the drought and the enclosed
story of the contest on Mt. Carmel. The establishment of Ahab
as villain rather than hero actually qualifies him to become
hero in a new sense, to play his part in Yahweh's program. In
the new story, the villainy/lack is a negative exchange, or
mutual deprivation; Ahab has withdrawn his allegiance from
Yahweh, so Yahweh has withdrawn rain from Ahab. And this sets
up certain expectations of how the situation will be righted,
by mutual restoration. Ahab will restore his allegiance to
Yahweh, and Yahweh will restore rain to Ahab. But this will
require that the epistemological turning-point be for Ahab also the volitional turning-point. Now must come a combat, in
which Ahab's readiness to be hero will be tested. We are ready
for a combat in which he will (1) overthrow Baal, and (2) de-
liver the Israel he has misled. The text heightens these expectations in teasing detail. Elijah proposes a contract to
Ahab, and it is accepted ("Now therefore send . . . so Ahab
sent . . . "). It involves his exercising power both over the
prophets of Baal and over the people of Israel. But our expectations are quite disappointed; having cooperated in setting
the stage, Ahab completely disappears from the narrative while
the real combat goes forward!

2.   The combat on Mt. Carmel

2.1   Delineation and summary of the text

18:21-40 commends itself as the appropriate delineation for several reasons /7/. These verses contain everything
to do with the actual combat, and no more. It is precisely
they which lack the character Ahab, having only Elijah, the
people, and the prophets of Baal. And this section fits the
basic Proppian pattern, in that it moves from an initial situation, in which the people are "following" both Yahweh and Baal,
without choosing between them or even considering the question,
which is god (this is the "villainy"), to a final situation,
in which they acknowledge Yahweh alone as god, and seem at least
to begin to "follow" him. This is the achievement of the
text. How is it achieved? Elijah proposes a contract to the
people (vs. 21): follow the true god. This is refused; volition is not established. He proposes a second contract to the
people (vs. 23-24), that they sanction a contest to determine
who the true god is. This is accepted (vs. 24), and the contest
goes forward. Elijah proposes a contract to Yahweh (vss. 36-
37) to provide proof, in the terms of the contest, that he is
god (a similar proposal by Baal's prophets to Baal having
aborted). Elijah's contract is accepted, and the proof given
(vs. 38). The people make the appropriate acknowledgement (vs.
39). In a final episode (vs. 40), Elijah proposes yet another
contract to the people, to apprehend Baal's prophets. This is
accepted, the prophets are caught, and Elijah kills them.

2.2   The climax and the pivot of the combat story

2.21   The intuitive climax of the account of the combat is
in vss. 38-39: the falling of Yahweh's fire, and the people's
confession of him. Here also is, ostensibly, the epistemological turning-point, where the truth is revealed to the people
(cf. 2.322). But the story has another turning-point, in a
sense more important, in the people's acceptance of Elijah's
second contract (vs. 24b: "It is well spoken.") We may call
this the pivot of the story. After this, despite the heaping
up of narrative effects, there is no real narrative tension in
the sense of uncertainty about where the story is going. This
is the point of real decision, the volitional turning-point,
which ensures that the story will achieve its movement from
the initial to the final situation. What accounts for this

gap between the real pivot and the apparent climax? We suggest
that the text creates distance between will and knowledge, and
that this is its main point. The people's volition precedes
their knowledge of what the stakes are. Space is won for free-
dom, and this, as we shall see, redounds to the credit of the
people.

2.22   There are numerous indications, both narrative and
semantic, that vs. 24b is a turning-point for the people: before this, they are in various ways associated with Baal and
his prophets, afterwards with Yahweh and Elijah. First, the
occurrences of ᶜnh, "answer", arrange themselves in a scheme:
the people fail to answer (first contract, vs. 21), answer
(second contract, vs. 24); Baal fails to answer (vss. 26, 29),
Yahweh answers (cf. Elijah's "answer me", vs. 37). To express
this formulaically:

$$\frac{\text{answer}}{\text{not answer}} = \frac{\text{Yahweh}}{\text{Baal}}$$

Second, the people's indecision (vs. 21) is described by the
same verb, psh, used for the ineffectual ritual of Baal's prophets (vs. 26) /8/. Third, even an apparent "slip of the tongue"
points in the same direction. In vs. 24 Elijah calls Baal
"your god", where we expect, continuing the address to the people
in vs. 23, the use of the third person, "let them call on the
name of their god." Fourth, after once saying yes to Elijah,
the people are found constantly obedient to him, not only in
the final episode in vs. 40, but also in the details of Elijah's
preparation of the burn-offering (vss. 30, 34) /9/. Tromp (500)
aptly points to the several occurrences of the verb ngš, "draw
near"; in vs. 21, Elijah must make the approach, but in vs.
30, the people approach him (and he himself "draws near" to
Yahweh in vs. 36).

2.23   But why such complication at the beginning of the
story? Distance between will and knowledge would be even better
created if the people simply accepted Elijah's first approach!
Why the two contracts, and above all, what accounts for the
people's change of mind between vs. 21 and vs. 24? This is
the real mystery in the story; and in a sense it will remain a
mystery -- the mystery of free will! But it is through the
probing of these questions that the analysis will go forward;
for our conclusion will be that precisely these questions

cannot be answered from within the combat story itself, but
only from consideration of the enclosing narrative.

2.3   The three stages of the combat story

2.30   As the preceding remarks have shown, the story has not
two but three stages; the first contract and its failure, the
second contract and its success (pivot), Yahweh's action and the
acknowledgement of him (narrative climax). These stages can be
traced in the changing role of the people; they move, in Propp's
terms, from <u>villain</u> (vs. 21), to <u>helper</u> (providing the hero with
what he needs for the contest, vss. 24, 34), and finally to
<u>sharing the hero's own role</u>, in acting as punishers of the
villain (vs. 40). Our procedure will be to analyze the three
stages from a series of perspectives, and then to ask again
why a three-stage story is necessary.

2.31   Analysis of the three stages

2.311   The first perspective is that of the people's <u>willing-
ness to make a choice</u>. The second contract calls on them to
sanction a contest, but there is a further implication. Elijah's
challenge presupposes that there will be a winner -- the story
simply discards the logical possibilities that both deities,
or neither, may answer by fire -- and the people's acceptance
is also an acceptance of this supposition. They choose <u>choice</u>,
where in vs. 21 they tacitly chose <u>no choice</u>! They agree, whatever the result, no longer to sit on the fence! Hence the three
stages are: unwillingness to choose, willingness to choose,
and actually choosing.

2.312   The second perspective, and of major importance, is
the <u>symmetry of the choice</u> offered to the people. The terms
of the first contract are completely <u>symmetrical</u> -- the choice
between Yahweh and Baal is an <u>equal</u> one. In the second, this
symmetry has been broken to the extent that the one proposing
it, and issuing the challenge, has identified himself (vs. 22)
with one side, Yahweh's. Yet even here the <u>terms</u> of the contest remain symmetrical (again the wording of vss. 23-24a pre-
serves this) except that Baal has more partisans. After vs.
24, the narrative seems intent on <u>undermining</u> the symmetry from
which it set out. There are many detailed indications of this.
In addition to the placing of the people on the side of Elijah,
we may note the measures taken to make Yahweh's task harder

(vss. 34-35) /10/, the identification of Elijah's sacrifice with
Israel (vs. 31), and even Elijah's "encouragement" of the prophets of Baal (vs. 27). To the three stages in the story correspond, in the choice between Yahweh and Baal, complete symmetry,
a symmetry broken but still in operation, and a symmetry prac-
tically abandoned.

2.313   The third perspective is that of the people's knowledge, of the stakes and of the outcome. The truth, as we have
said, is not made known to the people until the end of the story.
But, in a peculiar sense, they have acquired knowledge already
at the second stage. Suppose, in response to the first contract, they had said, "Yes, we will follow the true god, but we
do not know which it is". Volition, without knowledge! Then
Elijah's second proposal, for a contest, would have met this
need: "This is how you can determine which is the true god" /11/.
But instead, acquiring knowledge of how choice might be made
establishes, here in the actual story, the will to choose! The
normal sequence, will → knowledge, is reversed. But we must go
further. This knowledge comes from a prophet of Yahweh (vs. 22).
The people learn not only how a choice between Yahweh and Baal
might be made, but also that, of the two contestants, it is
Yahweh who demands choice and desires a contest. Yahweh is on
the side of choice, so that, even at this point in the story,
to choose choice is to choose Yahweh. Thus the three stages
of the people's story correspond, in terms of knowledge of what
the outcome will be, to no knowledge, implicit knowledge, explicit knowledge.

2.314   At the first stage, the people, ignorant of the stakes,
fail to choose between symmetrical alternatives. At the second,
having acquired implicit knowledge of the outcome, they agree
to make a choice; here the narrative maintains symmetry in the
terms of the contest, but breaks it in other ways. At the third
stage, the people receive a full revelation, and make a choice
which no longer is a real one; and the narrative has abandoned
all semblance of symmetry. This intricate discussion may be
summarized in diagrammatic form:

Vss.	Role of the people	Choice	Symmetry	Knowledge
21a			**Symmetry**	
21b	Villain	Unwillingness to choose		None
22-24a			**Broken Symmetry**	
24b	Helper	Willingness to choose		Implicit
25-37			**Symmetry abandoned**	
38-40	≃ Hero	Choice		Explicit

2.32   The necessity of the three stages

2.321   We may now press further the question raised earlier:
why a three-stage story, when a two-stage story would better
establish the <u>main point</u> (2.21), that the people <u>decided</u> before
they <u>knew</u>? Even the <u>implicit</u> knowledge of stage two tends to
negate this. One might surmise that the story is under some
pressure to tone down the credit which it does to the people.
But another approach is worth exploring, that the story must
made a second "point", in conflict with the main one; namely,
that the choice confronting the people at the beginning <u>was a</u>
<u>completely</u> <u>equal</u> <u>one</u> (as the symmetry of the choice suggests).
But this assertion leads to a logical and theological paradox.
Choice can be free only when it is unbiased, when it is between
symmetrical alternatives. But between totally symmetrical alternatives there is no basis for choice -- any basis for choice
is a bias! In theological form, this might read: one cannot
choose a god who coerces choice, but a god who cannot coerce
choice is not worth choosing! Confronted with <u>symmetry</u> between Yahweh and Baal, how can the people answer (vs. 21)?
Before they can, the story must be got "off centre", which is,
we hypothesize, what vss. 22-24a achieve. But how real is
their choice then? Are they not acting under constraint?

2.322   In an earlier chapter we discussed extensively the
function and the technique of one section of biblical narrative
in the face of a contradiction of which both sides must be
affirmed (I.3.24). In the present case, the contradiction may
be expressed as follows:

> 1. Israel has no basis for choice between Baal
>   and Yahweh, but
>
> 2. Israel unconstrainedly chooses Yahweh.

The first half of the contradiction tends to collapse stages two
and three of the story into each other -- the people "choose"
Yahweh as the true god only after he becomes known to them as
the true god, so that there is no real choice. The second half
of the contradiction tends to collapse stages one and two --
the choice was made at the very beginning of the story, and confirmed only at the end. The narrative as we have it has brought
stages one and two as close together as possible, so that the
people's change of mind is very sudden and unaccountable, while
stretching stages two and three as far as possible apart. And
perhaps above all, it so stresses the acquisition of explicit
knowledge at the end as to distract the mind from the acquisition of implicit knowledge in the middle. The wording of vss.
36-37 is significant in this respect: " . . . let it be known
. . . that I am thy servant, and that I have done all these
things at thy word," and " . . . that this people may know
that thou . . . hast turned their hearts back." Now, nothing
could be more conspicuous than the initiative that Elijah has
taken all through the story. He has proposed all the contracts,
even to Yahweh! Only at the very end comes the twist -- despite
appearances, it was Yahweh all the time /12/!

2.323   All of these points about the present form of the
story justify our assumption that it is the second term of the
contradiction which is the main point, while the first term
is narratively a disruptive element. But we have now come as
far as an internal analysis of the combat story can bring us.
In its present form, it is under a powerful constraint to
affirm that the people were in no position to choose, when
they came to Mt. Carmel, between Yahweh and Baal. But why it
is under this constraint will only appear from a consideration
of the "exchange of meaning" between the combat and drought
stories (3.2). But before we can move to the relationships
between the stories, two important points must be added.

2.4   Addenda to the analysis of the combat story

2.41   First, the program of the combat story, "revealed"
only by the final twist in the narrative to which we have just
referred (2.322), though implicitly clear to the reader throughout, is, in Greimas's scheme:

$$
\begin{array}{ccc}
\text{Yahweh} \longrightarrow & \text{Israel's} \longrightarrow & \text{Yahweh} \\
 & \text{allegiance} & \\
 & \uparrow & \\
\text{Elijah} \longrightarrow & \text{Israel} &
\end{array}
$$

2.42   Second, we have thus far made little reference to the
prophets of Baal. Elijah's contract with the people to sanction
a contest implies a subsequent contract between the people and
the prophets of Baal. Elijah implies that the people can make
Baal's prophets enter the contest, and the story implies that
this was done. The important point is that the people here
"dominate" Baal's prophets. In this light, vs. 40 can be seen
as a heightened reprise of the earlier incident -- in each case
the people put the prophets in an appropriate situation, and
Elijah overcomes them there. But vs. 40 still presents something of a problem, for nothing in the combat story has led us
to expect the death penalty for the losers! We shall return
to this problem (3.211).

3.   The two stories as one unit

3.0   The "natural" relationship between the accounts of the
drought and of the combat on Mt. Carmel -- the relationship
given, as it were, by the text itself -- is a sequential, or
syntagmatic, relationship. But certain parallels between the
analyses of the two stories invite also a paradigmatic analysis, comparing the two side by side (for the terminology, cf.
II.1.0). This proves, in fact, to be a most productive step.

3.1   Paradigmatic analysis

3.11   The narrative programs determined for the two stories
(1.322, 2.41) are, except in one particular, identical:

Yahweh ————→ Israel's ————→ Yahweh
                allegiance
                    ↑
Elijah ————————→ x

In the drought story, x = Ahab, and in the combat story, x =
Israel. This suggests that the stories effect a comparison between Ahab and the people, in which the term of comparison is
their responses to Elijah (and, thereby, to Yahweh).

3.12   The essentials of the comparison are given in the
following table:

	The drought (Elijah and Ahab)	The combat (Elijah and the people)
First approach of Elijah	17:1	18:21a
Its failure	implicit	18:21b
Second approach of Elijah	18:17-19	18:22-24a
Provides knowledge	explicit (epistemological turning-point)	implicit
Demands domination of Baal prophets	18:19	18:23-24a
Its success	18:20 (volitional turning-point)	18:24b (volitional turning-point)
Various minor contracts	18:41-42	18:30
accepted	18:44-45	18:34
		explicit knowledge 18:38 (epistemological turning-point)
		fulfillment of initial contract 18:39-40

The rest of the analysis is a commentary on this table.

3.131   In the face of an existing fault, Elijah makes in
each case an approach which is without consequence; in this
respect 17:1 may be compared with 18:21, for, though no explicit
"contract" is proposed to Ahab, and though he is not
specifically said to have "not answered", his lack of response
to so urgent a threat is striking. In each case, we have argued,
the initial fault involved ignorance of the true stakes.
This ignorance accounts for the failure of Elijah's first
approach -- Ahab's initiative in 18:3-16 is still based on his
misconception of the situation -- so that when the prophet
makes a second approach he in each case conveys knowledge,
and has better success. In each case, this second approach
is the volitional turning-point for the protagonists, who
accept a contract (involving domination of the prophets of
Baal!), and who thereafter accept all the minor contracts
which Elijah proposes to them (18:30, 34, cf. vss. 41-42,
44-45).

3.132   There is thus impressive parallelism, but there are
also differences, which in every case show the people in a
better light than their king. Where Ahab's fault is apostasy
(18:18), the people's is only syncretism (though admittedly
the story goes on to deny that syncretism is really possible).
The people's volition is as free as possible, but Ahab's is
little different from obligation (he knows he must cooperate
in order to secure rain); for the people, the turning-point
of knowledge (vs. 39) comes after that of volition (previously
they have had at most an implicit knowledge), whereas for Ahab
they coincide. Above all, it is the people's repentance only
which is carried through, and it is they who bring to its conclusion
the "domination" of the prophets of Baal.

3.2   Syntagmatic analysis

3.20   We shall consider in turn what each of the two stories
contributes to the meaning of the other by their being in just
their present sequence.

3.21   The combat and its context

3.211   The combat story requires, at the most superficial
level, an occasion; and this is provided by 18:19-20, in which
the actors are gathered and the initial situation set up.
These verses belong, in fact, to both the enclosed and the

enclosing story; Ahab acts in them as part of his story, but
thereby begins a story in which he pointedly has no part /13/.
At the other end of the combat account, vs. 40 has been the
subject of considerable debate; is it part of, or an addition
to, the main account /14/? From our standpoint, though this
verse has something to contribute to the narrative logic of the
combat story (2.42), it does not really belong to it, and should
be seen primarily in terms of the exchange of meaning with the
context; the killing of the prophets is **quid pro quo** in relation
to Jezebel's killing of Yahweh's prophets. More generally, the
context provides a larger framework for the conflict between
Yahweh and Baal and explains the numerical disproportion between Yahweh's and Baal's prophets, in that Jezebel has perse-
cuted the one and nurtured the other.

3.212   But the combat story requires from its context something more profound. The major point which emerged from our
analysis of this story was, why it needed so badly to affirm
Israel's inability to choose between Yahweh and Baal, a need
which occasioned logical problems as well as narrative compli-
cations. The answer, we now suggest, lies in the need to demonstrate to what a pass Ahab's leadership has brought his
people! Before vs. 21, where we learn of the people's indecision, there has been no mention of their apostasy, but only
of Ahab's. Israel's "villainy" is the result of the king's
prior villainy -- if they are unable to tell the difference
between Yahweh and Baal, it is his doing!

3.22   The drought and its enclosure

          Conversely, the combat story supplies to the drought
story, at exactly the right point, the Proppian combat sequence.
But it does so in a pointedly "wrong" way, completely replacing
Ahab, as hero, by the people. If their fault is really his,
then the reversal of the fault is not his, but theirs! Ahab's
story is interrupted just at the point where he might repent
and act as the hero. In fact, he even "passes" the small test
which Elijah sets him, in setting up the combat. But he has
no share in the decisive event. He simply reaps the benefit,
obtaining the rain he sought. That he has kingly power over
the people is merely an irony; he is their leader in apostasy,
but not in returning!

3.3   Summary of the analysis

3.31   What we have done in this analysis is, we hope, of
some methodological significance. We were initially confronted
with a story enclosed in another story, each conforming to a
general definition of a well-formed narrative. This phenomenon
of enclosure is typical in biblical narrative, whereas it is not,
for example, in the literature out of which Propp created his
theories. Like one sentence in a paragraph, to return to the
linguistic analogy (0.1), a biblical story exists in an inter-
dependent relationship with its context. How can a precise
understanding of this relationship be gained when the available theoretical models deal almost exclusively with the discrete story?

3.32   Our procedure has been, first, to wrench the stories
apart in an artificial way, and to enquire closely into the
meaning of each (1, 2); then, to force them into an artificial
relationship to each other (the paradigmatic analysis, 3.1);
and finally, to demand, as it were, what each wanted from the
other (the syntagmatic analysis, 3.2). To use an analogy, we
first determined the "meaning" to be exchanged, then converted
it into a common currency, and finally observed the actual pro-
cess of exchange.

3.33   By these means, we have arrived at a new synthesis,
with a maximized awareness of the exchange of meaning between
the parts. Though 1 Kg 17-18 belongs traditionally to an
"Elijah Cycle", the prophet is only a catalyst for the message
of these chapters. His role never changes, so that the parts
he plays cancel each other out, exposing the true object of
discourse (and is it not indeed the role of the prophet to
disappear, and to reveal the true object of discourse!) The
true object is the relationship between Ahab and the people
of Israel, about which almost nothing is said directly! And
the message is that the king is decidedly worse than useless;
inferior to the people (paradigmatic analysis), he leads them
into apostasy and lags behind in repentance (syntagmatic analysis).

4.   Appendices

4.0   The foregoing analysis is, within the limited terms
of reference (0.1-2), complete. In what follows, we sketch

the lines along which it invites further development, towards
the comprehensive reading at which we aimed in Chapter II.

4.1   Narrative analysis of the drought story

4.10   In analyzing the drought sequence, we confined the
discussion to the essentials of the Proppian pattern; and, of
the three large sub-stories enclosed within it, we chose to
analyze only one, that of the combat on Mt. Carmel, in relation to the whole. The sub-stories largely neglected were
those of Elijah and the widow (17:8-24), and of Obadiah (18:
3-16).

4.11   Syntagmatically, these two stories function, as we
have seen, to anticipate the reversal of the Ahab-quest story
into the Ahab-villainy story, which is formally accomplished
by 18:17-18 (1.23, 1.31). Both, that is, call in question the
identification of Ahab as hero and Elijah as villain. The
Obadiah story, like the combat story, undermines the expected
Proppian sequence, as it were, from within; it provides, at
just the right point, the "qualification" sequence of Ahab's
quest (0.311), with Obadiah as "helper". But it does so in a
way which seems to cast doubt on Ahab's fitness for the role
of hero. The story of Elijah and the widow does not fit the
Proppian sequence; and indeed, only its first part (17:8-16)
clearly has the drought as its backdrop. It serves the purpose of displaying the "villain" Elijah in a favorable light
before the "hero" Ahab even takes up his quest; yet we feel
dissatisfaction with this as an explanation of its function /15/.

4.12   Paradigmatically, we may sketch the outlines of what
certainly would be a productive paralleling of these two sub-
stories with the combat story and with the drought sequence as
a whole. In 17:8-16 and 18:7-16, Elijah proposes contracts in
the familiar way. In the case of Obadiah, we see again the
prophet's double approach (3.12), with first negative and then
postive results. Alone of all those whom Elijah confronts in
1 Kg 17-18, the widow responds positively to his initial approach (17:11a), and even she then hesitates (vs. 12) before
finally obeying (vss 15). The opposition volition vs. knowledge, so important in our earlier analysis, is in play in
these two stories; the widow responds willingly to Elijah
long before she knows the truth about him, while Obadiah,
though recognizing Elijah instantly (18:7), hesitates to obey

him. The second part of the story of the widow (17:17-24)
differs from all that we have previously considered, in that
it begins with _her_ confronting Elijah. But perhaps there is
something worth exploring in the odd elements of parallelism
between this section and 18:17-40: (i) an accusation against
Elijah (17:18; 18:17); (ii) the accusation turned onto Yahweh
(17:20), back onto Ahab (18:18); (iii) a miracle operated
through Elijah; (iv) a recognition (17:24; 18:39).

4.2   Semantic analysis of the drought story

4.20   What first attracted our attention to the problem of
the relationship between the drought and combat sequences was,
in fact, the possibilities for _semantic_ analysis (cf. II.2),
inherent above all in the opposition fire/water. But the narrative analysis demanded precedence (here we disagree with the
opinion of Polzin: 14, that "there is no _a priori_ hierarchical
order of analysis of a given text"), and proved to be worth a
study of its own. Our narrative analysis has not, of course,
been devoid of semantic considerations (cf. especially 2.22),
for there never can be any such ultimate separation of the two
areas; but there has been no systematic discussion. We offer
here only the most general remarks, except in the case of
fire/water where our comments will be more substantial.

4.21   Among the recurrent elements with which a semantic
analysis would deal are _eating_ and _drinking_/_hunger_ and _thirst_
and _life_/_death_, and these come together particularly in connection with the treatment of prophets (killing/nurturing them).
The oppositions _Israelite_/_foreign_ and _male_/_female_ come together
in the foreign woman (cf. II.2.221, where the issue was instigation to sin). _Division_ and _choice_ (between two alternatives) are recurrent (18:6, 21, 23, 25, and cf. our discussion
in 2.311), and will gain in importance when we move to the
larger context (16:21, on which cf. 4.32). The _geographical_
code (cf. II.2.21) appears to be of special importance, for
"Elijah chose Baal's own ground to defy him" (Montgomery: 304),
perhaps in the combat on Mt. Carmel, and certainly in his move
to Sidon (17:9). Most of the semantic categories we have
enumerated are well represented in the story of Elijah and
the widow, and we intuit that it is at the semantic level of
analysis that the function of this story (left rather ambiguous
by the narrative analysis) can be best accounted for.

4.221   The question of "fire and water" in 1 Kg 17-18 has
been the object of extensive debate, and one recent study devoted to it (Tromp) adopts a literary approach not unrelated
to our own. But there is great confusion in the debate, and
the cause of it seems to be that many scholars, realizing the
need to bring all the references to fire and to water into some
connection with each other, have tried to do so in a literarily
illegitimate way. Specifically, they believe that rain is referred to, by implication, in 18:21-40; since the context is a
drought, and since the result is the coming of rain, it is held
that the combat on Mt. Carmel must really be about getting the
rain. There are two lines of argument. A considerable number
of scholars see in the ritual acts evidence of rain-making
ceremonies, though there is little agreement among them in detail /16/. Many more assume that the "fire of Yahweh" (18:38)
is lightning, the harbinger of rain /17/. What is in fact
taking place is a rain-making competition /18/.

4.222   If rain is referred to in 18:21-40, it is certainly
only by implication, and this fact in itself is of literary
importance. The section does not mention rain, though of
course it does mention water (vss. 34, 35). If rain-making
rituals are being used, this is significant; but in the sense
that we must ask why they are being used to make fire, which
mythologically is anti-rain! As to the "fire of Yahweh", the
text goes to some length to make clear that it precedes the
first appearance of cloud (vss. 43-44); and that it need not
be lightning is sufficiently shown by Num 11:1 (cf. our Chapter
II).

4.223   Analysis should begin from what seems to be the clear
semantic coherence of the text on this issue. Ahab, in the
drought story, comes to know Yahweh as withholder of water;
Israel, in the combat story, comes to know him as provider of
fire (anti-water). Elijah, who in ch. 17 gets water into his
possession ("except by my word", vs. 1) -- becomes, mythologically speaking,"master of water" -- is the one able to "offer"
water in ch. 18. Yahweh's consumption of this water-offering
is reprise and confirmation of his consuming of water through
the drought.

4.3   The larger context and the character Jezebel

4.30   The drought sequence is itself enclosed in some larger

unit. It will be possible to do no more than to suggest what
this is, and to make a very few remarks about it. Our procedure
is to ask what demands the drought story makes on its context;
what questions does it raise, but leave unanswered? In other
words, having extensively analyzed a text, with what expectations do we move to its context?

4.31   Of the people, we are at most left asking whether
their acknowledgement of Yahweh (18:39) will be carried through;
and perhaps even this question has been answered by their cooperation in the killing of the prophets of Baal (vs. 40). But
the role of Ahab has received no such resolution. His "quest"
has indeed been covered. But we expect to learn more about his
initial situation of apostasy, and about Jezebel's role in it;
it has been hinted (18:4, 13, 18-19) that she instigated it /19/.
And at the end of Ahab's quest, we do not know at all whether
he will follow Yahweh or Baal, side with Israel or with Jezebel.
In the case of Elijah, our expectations are of a different kind.
We have seen him in an unchanging, catalytic role, and we expect the context to give us more of the same (or even to lack
him entirely, for Old Testament prophets do come and go sud-
denly and unaccountably!) Putting the last two points together,
we might expect that, if Elijah does appear in the larger context, he will overcome Jezebel there, completing a series of
"layers" in which his domination of the people (combat story)
is enclosed in his domination of Ahab, instigator of the people
(drought story), which is enclosed in his domination of Jezebel,
instigator of Ahab (larger context).

4.32   As it turns out, the context largely disappoints such
expectations but does so in a strikingly systematic way! The
people disappear as an active "character" in ch. 19; nor are
they involved in the prior career of Ahab (16:29-34). But if
we go back further in ch. 16, we find that "all Israel made
Omri king" (vs. 16), and, even more importantly, that "the
people of Israel were divided into two parts; half of the people
followed Tibni ben Ginath, and half followed Omri" (vs. 21).
Caught between two opinions! In accordance with our expectations, 16:29-34 introduces Ahab in his apostasy to Baal, and
as having married Jezebel.   At the end, he returns directly to
her, and nothing good is said of him before his not too distant
death. Of Jezebel's prior story, more curiously, the prior
narrative says nothing; her persecution of Yahweh's prophets,
and her hypothetical instigation of Ahab's apostasy, deduced

from ch. 18, get only indirect confirmation in 16:29-34. But
immediately _after_ ch. 18, she is revealed again in her role as
killer of prophets of Yahweh, threatening the life of Elijah
(19:2). In the case of _Elijah_ himself the context has a real
surprise for us. Before 17:1, it tells nothing of his origin --
his appearance there is extremely abrupt -- but in ch. 19 it
makes a real character of him, a "personality" subject to
changes. He undergoes his own story, rather than merely pre-
siding over the stories of others. We find him alone, express-
ing fear, the wish for death, and even paranoia. Above all,
we are quickly disabused of the notion that he will dominate
Jezebel. On the contrary, she dominates him, and is the cause
of his "passion" /20/!

4.33   There are two main points to be made from these findings. First, although the hint that Jezebel is the instigator
of Ahab will receive confirmation _later_ (especially in the notice
of Ahab's death, 21:25), it receives none from the narrative
preceding the drought story. On the contrary, 16:15-34 taken
as a whole actually reverses the order of instigation to sin
(Jezebel $\longrightarrow$ Ahab $\longrightarrow$ Israel) posited from chs. 17-18; for
Israel takes the initiative in Omri's rise to power, and by implication causes Ahab's kingship, while _Ahab_ takes the initiative in marrying Jezebel. Second, Jezebel's domination of
Elijah, and his consequent change of role, lead directly to
his being instructed to anoint the triumvirate of Hazael, Jehu,
and Elisha. It is surely no coincidence that all three of
these will outlive Jezebel, and the whole Omride dynasty, while
Elijah will not, though he will outlive Ahab! Both of these
points suggest, and it is here that we shall close our analysis, that the most fruitful "larger context" in which to view
1 Kg 17-18 is neither the Ahab nor the Elijah traditions, but
the cycle covering the rise and fall of the House of Omri
(1 Kg 16:15-2 Kg 10:27) /21/.

FOOTNOTES TO CHAPTER III

/1/   In the usage we have adopted, "helper" has analogous
meanings in the two schemes.

/2/   Smend (535-36) discusses the possibility of an originally separate drought story, consisting of elements of 1 Kg 17-
18, but finds considerable difficulties with the various

reconstructions of it which have been proposed. Nonetheless, there is a striking convergence between these reconstructions and our "Ahab-quest" story (1.21).

/3/   Structural analysis often procedes by considering the imaginable alternatives to the given text; e.g. Crossan (200-201).

/4/   On the question of initiative in 18:3-15, cf. Tromp (489).

/5/   On the problems of this final section in relation to what precedes, cf. Smend (especially 535-36).

/6/   This is the meaning of ᶜkr certainly in Jos 6:18, 7:25, Judg 11:35, and 1 Chr 2:7, and perhaps also in Gen 34:30 and 1 Sam 14:29 (on the last, Jobling, 1976: 370).

/7/   For discussions of the delineation, Smend (537-38) and Tromp (488-91). Against those who argue for the original unity of ch. 18 or of some even larger section, both insist that the no doubt impressive unity of the final form is the result of extensive redaction (Tromp: "A structure may be secondary as well as splendid" [488]). Our view is that the combat story displays clear evidence of both its original separateness from, and its scrupulous incorporation into, its present context.

/8/   The precise meaning of psh is unclear. The tradition-al "limp" has no obvious connection with indecision. Some kind of ritual dancing is clearly involved. See the discussions in Gray (1963: 352-53) and de Vaux (240-41).

/9/   Following the Hebrew verse-division, in which the RSV's vs. 33b is the beginning of vs. 34.

/10/   For a discussion of the various views of the significance of these two verses, cf. Tromp (486-87).

/11/   For the technique of trying out alternative stories, cf. 1.21.

/12/   Tromp's discussion (493) converges with ours on this point.

/13   On 18:19-20, cf. especially Würthwein (132).

/14/   Smend (537-38), Würthwein (134), and Tromp (494),
offer valuable, and divergent, points of view.

/15/   There remains another "syntagmatic" issue, the extraordinary use of the "flashback" in the Obadiah story. The question belongs partly in a discussion of the larger context (4.3),
since some of the references are to Jezebel's villainy (18:4,
13); while these verses certainly function to identify Obadiah
himself, it is surely more important that, without them, we would
know nothing of Jezebel's persecution of the prophets! But
there is more to the "flashbacks" than this; Obadiah's statement in vs. 10 is essential to the reconstruction of the Ahab-
quest story itself (1.21)! Is the point, perhaps, to downgrade
Ahab's role as hero by referring to it thus indirectly?

/16/   Tromp (482-84) provides a comprehensive summary of the
arguments. Cf. also Ap-Thomas (152-53).

/17/   Again, a summary of views in Tromp (484-85). Cf.
Ap-Thomas (150-54).

/18/   Against this whole approach, cf. Smend (537) and especially Würthwein (136-39). Tromp's final position (494-95) is
what he calls "conciliatory", but seems to us not an adequate
account of the text as it stands.

/19/   The relation between text and context differs here
from what it was in the case of the combat and the drought. It
was only in moving from the combat to its context that we learned
that the people's fault was instigated by Ahab; the combat story
contained no hint of this, nor indeed any reference to Ahab.

/20/   On the abruptness of 17:1, and on the failure of the
preceding narrative adequately to "set the scene" for the
drought, cf. Smend (534-35). Cf. also his discussion (525) of
the relation of ch. 19 to chs. 17-18.

/21/   This fits well with the remarks of Smend (538-40).

Postscript

> There is no real end to mythological analysis . . . .
> Themes can be split up ad infinitum. Just when you
> think you have disentangled and separated them, you
> realize that they are knitting together again in re-
> sponse to the operation of unexpected affinities.
> Consequently the unity of the myth is never more than
> tendential and projective . . . . It is a phenomenon
> of the imagination, resulting from the attempt at in-
> terpretation; . . . there is always something left
> unfinished (Lévi-Strauss, 1969: 5-6).

1.   Retrospect

1.1   A short time ago, these studies could not have been
written. That they have been written, and may even be read, is
a measure of the rapid rise of "biblical structuralism" (borrow-
ing the title of Robert Polzin's recent book). So my first
feeling is of gratitude for the permission to study biblical
texts in such experimental ways. Worthwhile results are achieved
by such studies, which could not have been achieved by traditional
methods. They raise problematic issues, and leave unanswered
questions, some of which will be taken up here. But the most
important justification for these analyses must be, simply, the
exegetical gains.

1.2   Theoretical discussion of structuralism in general,
and of biblical structuralism in particular, continues to pro-
liferate (cf., very recently, Polzin and Detweiler); as indeed
it must. Some of this discussion raises questions about the
validity of my analyses (e.g. Lévi-Strauss's reservations about
the application of his theories to Old Testament; Leach: 25-31).
The narrative models of Greimas, upon which I have based so
much, have been under methodological fire (Detweiler: 119-21,
with references). But I believe that, in biblical structuralism, theory has outweighed practice to an unjustifiable extent,

and I have worked at redressing the balance. Theoretical criticism of methods should, after all, be based on a full understanding of what can be achieved with them in practice!

1.3   I am sensitive, on the other hand, to the doubts about
structural exegesis among historical-critical exegetes, especially since I myself have been trained as one. Though many voices
have expressed the need for rapprochement, or at least debate,
between the two sides, I know of no really valuable attempt to
begin it (though the discussion by Patte: 1-20 brings us to the
threshold). I have not myself, in these analyses, entered into
such a debate with historical-critical exegesis, but I have at
least kept in touch with it. My analysis of "Jonathan" led me
to historical conclusions (albeit negative ones) about this biblical character (I.3.33), and there may be a basis here for
meaningful debate /1/. And in Chapter III I made a special
point of referring to other studies, particularly of form, tradition, and redaction, whose interests converged with mine.
Certainly in locating those textual phenomena which demand explanation, and in delineating the appropriate text for analysis,
I rarely fail to benefit, as I prepare a structural study, from
any careful analysis based on any method. To this extent, at
least, there can already be a productive relationship between
structural and historical-critical exegesis.

2.   Prospect

2.0   It was not my intention, as I began the analyses in
Chapters II and III, that they be so open-ended as they now
appear -- each ends with a section on "Where shall we go next?"
But this sense that any "whole" represents merely an arbitrary
halting-place is profoundly a part of the structuralist ethos --
the analysis never ends! Looking at the chapters of this book
together, I am aware of two directions in which they point to
need for future work. And these two directions correspond yet
again to the categories "paradigm" and "syntagm" which have re-
curred so frequently through these pages.

2.1   Paradigm: Systematic relations between
           discrete biblical narratives

2.10   At many levels, these analyses have thrown up features
common to different sections of Old Testament narrative. The

following are offered merely as examples of the rich variety of possibilities for continuing paradigmatic study.

2.11   The passages gathered together in II.4 shared with Num 11-12 and with each other numerous __small elements of meaning__ (words, phrases, themes), which seemed to be recombined in different ways from one passage to another. Analysis based on such elements is characteristic of Lévi-Strauss, and its potential for biblical studies seems to me enormous.

2.12   Both in Chapter II and in Chapter III, we met with the phenomenon of __instigation__ (to sin), in which one character brought about the action of another; in Chapter II, this proved to have a systematic relationship to the theme of punishment (II.1.3), which would probably have been the case also in Chapter III had the issue been pursued there. Here we have a case of a __narrative type__, with apparent implications for meaning, which could be investigated in many Old Testament passages from the Garden of Eden on! Such an approach, with relationships to form- and genre-analysis, but of greater generality, is characteristic of Greimas. It would proceed by working out typologies of such recurrent narrative types.

2.13   The most compelling recurrent feature of all three analyses is surely __knowledge__; what is really going on in the story, who knows it, and how is it made known? This is a case of a __major isotopy__ (cf. II.0.3, II.2.1) linking the three analyses -- and not only these, for knowledge is of similar central importance, to mention but one example, in Polzin's recent analysis of the Book of Job (54-125; e.g. 105: at the end of the book "good fortune is possessed with insight (by Job and by the reader) whereas . . . Job's blessings at the beginning were without such insight"). Systematic study of the modes of occurrence of this isotopy in Old Testament narratives would provide a new basis for the understanding, for instance, of "revelation".

2.2   Syntagm: Approaching biblical narrative
        in its large pieces

Biblical narrative is given to us, for the most part, in very large continuous pieces. Few models for the structural analysis of such long narratives are, however, available from outside of biblical studies (but cf. the attempts discussed by

Detweiler: 145-58). Within biblical studies, the following
cover very large sequential units: Leach on "The Legitimacy of
Solomon" (25-83), Polzin on Job (54-125), and the forthcoming
dissertation by E. S. Malbon on the Gospel of Mark, of which a
sample is available (Malbon). But none of these have as their
main concern the sort of narrative analysis attempted here. In
Chapter I the analysis was attempted, though schematically, of
a unit consisting of many chapters of 1 Samuel; and in an appendix to Chapter III (III.4.3) the beginning was sketched of
an analysis of a unit in the Books of Kings, of comparable
length. The whole discussion, in Chapter III, of the "exchange
of meaning" between text and context opens the way to the analysis of longer narratives.

2.3   Where shall we go next?

2.31   The preceding remarks have pointed to a need which is
very great in the field of structural exegesis -- the precise
definition of tasks. Not surprisingly, the newly available
methods have been applied by various exegetes to various parts
of the Old Testament, and striking results have been obtained.
But if a point of diminishing returns is not to be reached, it
seems to me that collaborative work towards agreed goals will be
necessary. This is beginning in the Consultation on Structuralism and Biblical Exegesis of the Society of Biblical Literature.

2.32   For my own part, I see the most pressing need to be
syntagmatic, and my long-term project is a structural approach
to the Deuteronomic History. The method I envisage combines
working outwards from analysis of limited sections (cf. Chapters I and III here) with working inwards from a preliminary
model of the whole. Such a model can be based on the major
divisions of the History marked by the passages which (according to Noth, 1943: 3-12, and McCarthy, 1965) are deliberately
supplied by the deuteronomists to organize the work. More
studies towards this long-term goal may be expected soon.

FOOTNOTE TO THE POSTSCRIPT

/1/   In the forthcoming publication mentioned in II /16/ I
investigate the still almost universal judgment that I Sam 11 is
the "most nearly historical" account of Saul's rise to kingship;
not trying to "prove" its untenability, but suggesting that
historians ask whether it is compatible with the literary data.

Works Consulted

Ackroyd, P. R.   *The First Book of Samuel*. The Cambridge
    1971   Bible Commentary. Cambridge: University
               Press.

Ap-Thomas, D. R.   "Elijah on Mount Carmel". PEQ 92: 146-55.
    1960

Barthes, R.   *Critical Essays*. Trans. by R. Howard.
    1972   Evanston: Northwestern University Press.

    1974   *Et al.*, *Structural Analysis and Biblical
               Exegesis*. Trans. by A. M. Johnson, Jr.
               Pittsburgh: Pickwick Press.

Birch, B. C.   *The Rise of the Israelite Monarchy: The
    1976   Growth and Development of 1 Samuel 7-15*.
               Missoula, Montana: Scholars Press.

Calloud, J.   "Apocalypse 12:13: Essai d'analyse sémiot-
    1976a   ique". *Foi et vie*, *Cahiers bibliques* 15:
               26-78.

    1976b   *Structural Analysis of Narrative*. Trans. by
               D. Patte. Philadelphia: Fortress Press.

Calvin, J.   *Commentaries on the Four Last Books of Moses
    1950   Arranged in the Form of a Harmony*. Volume
               4. Grand Rapids: Eerdmans.

Coats, G. W.   *Rebellion in the Wilderness*. Nashville:
    1968   Abingdon Press.

Conrad, J.   *Die junge Generation im alten Testament*.
    1970   Stuttgart: Calwer Verlag.

Crespy, G.   "The Parable of the Good Samaritan: An
    1974   Essay in Structural Research". *Semeia*
               2:27-50.

Crossan, J. D.   "Structuralist Analysis and the Parables
      1974   of Jesus". Semeia 1: 192-221.

Culler J.   Ferdinand de Saussure. New York: Penguin
      1977   Books.

Culley, R. C.   "Structural Analysis: Is it Done with
      1974   Mirrors?" Int 28: 165-181.

      1976   Studies in the Structure of Hebrew Narrative.
                        Philadelphia: Fortress Press.

De George, R. T.   The Structuralists from Marx to Lévi-Strauss.
  and F. M., eds.   Garden City, New York: Doubleday.
      1972

De Vaux, R.   "The Prophets of Baal on Mount Carmel". The
      1971   Bible and the Ancient Near East. Trans. by
                        D. McHugh. Garden City, New York: Double-
                        day: 238-51.

De Vries, S. J.   "David's Victory over the Philistine as
      1973   Saga and as Legend". JBL 92: 23-36.

Detweiler, R.   Story, Sign and Self: Phenomenology and
      1978   Structuralism as Literary Critical Methods.
                        Philadelphia: Fortress Press.

Edwardsen, M.   Sartrean Analysis and Biblical Exegesis: An
      1977   Interpretation of Numbers 11 and 12. Unpub-
                        lished S.T.M. thesis, Union Theological
                        Seminary, New York.

Eerdmans, B. D.   "The Composition of Numbers". Oudtestament-
      1949   ische Studiën 6: 101-216.

Gibson, A. B.   The Religion of Dostoevsky. Philadelphia:
      1973   The Westminster Press.

Ginzberg, L.   The Legends of the Jews. 7 vols. Philadel-
      1909-38   phia: Jewish Publication Society of America.

Gray, G. B.   A Critical and Exegetical Commentary on
      1903   Numbers. ICC. New York: Scribner's.

Gray, J.   I & II Kings: A Commentary. Philadelphia:
      1963   The Westminster Press.

Greimas, A. J.   Sémantique structurale: Recherche de méthode.
      1966   Paris: Larousse.

      1970   De sens: Essais sémiotiques. Paris: Edi-
                      tions du Seuil.

      1971a   "The Interpretation of Myth: Theory and
                      Practice". Structural Analysis of Oral
                      Tradition, ed. by P. and E. K. Maranda.
                      Philadelphia: University of Pennsylvania
                      Press: 81-121. (Translation of 1970: 185-
                      230).

      1971b   "Narrative Grammar: Units and Levels".
                      MLN 86: 793-806.

      1973a   "Les actants, les acteurs et les figures".
                      C. Chabrol, et al., Sémiotique narrative
                      et textuelle. Paris: Larousse: 161-76.

      1973b   "Un problème de sémiotique narrative: Les
                      objets de valeur". Langages 31:13-35.

Grønbaek, J. H.   Die Geschichte vom Aufsteig Davids (1 Sam.
      1971   15-2 Sam. 5): Tradition und Komposition.
                      Copenhagen: Munksgaard.

Hertzberg, H. W.   I and II Samuel: A Commentary. Trans. by
      1964   J. S. Bowden. Philadelphia: The Westmin-
                      ster Press.

Jacobson, R.   "The Structuralists and the Bible". Int
      1974   28: 146-64.

Jobling, D.   "Saul's Fall and Jonathan's Rise: Tradi-
      1976   tion and Redaction in 1 Samuel 14:1-46".
                      JBL 95: 367-76.

      1978   Review of Polzin (below) forthcoming in
                      Union Seminary Quarterly Review.

Keil, C. F. and   Biblical Commentary on the Old Testament.
     F. Delitzsch   Volume 3. Grand Rapids: Eerdmans.
     n.d.

Lane, M., ed.   Introduction to Structuralism. New York:
     1970   Basic Books.

Leach, E.   Genesis as Myth and Other Essays. London:
     1969   Jonathan Cape.

Lévi-Strauss, C.   Structural Anthropology. Trans. by C.
     1963   Jacobson and B. G. Schoepf. New York:
                       Basic Books.

     1969   The Raw and the Cooked. Trans. by J. and
                       D. Weightman. New York: Harper & Row.

     1973   From Honey to Ashes. Trans. by J. and D.
                       Weightman. New York: Harper & Row.

McCarthy, D. J.   "II Samuel 7 and the Structure of the
     1965   Deuteronomic History". JBL 84: 131-38.

     1973   "The Inauguration of Monarchy in Israel:
                       A Form-Critical Study of I Samuel 8-12".
                       Int 27: 401-12.

Malbon, E. S.   "Elements of an Exegesis of the Gospel of
     1977   Mark According to Lévi-Strauss' Methodology".
                       Society of Biblical Literature Seminar
                       Papers: 155-70.

Montgomery, J. A.   A Critical and Exegetical Commentary on
     1951   the Books of Kings. ICC. New York:
                       Scribner's.

Morgenstern, J.   "David und Jonathan". JBL 78: 322-25.
     1959

Noth, M.   Überlieferungsgeschichtliche Studien.
     1943   I. Die sammelnden und bearbeitenden
                       Geschichtswerke im alten Testament. Halle:
                       Max Niemeyer.

Noth, M.   *Numbers: A Commentary*. Trans. by J. D.
       1968   Martin. Philadelphia: Westminster.

       1972   *A History of Pentateuchal Traditions*. Trans.
                   by B. W. Anderson. Englewood Cliffs, New
                   Jersey: Prentice Hall.

Num(bers) R(abba) *Midrash Rabbah: Numbers*. Trans. by J. J.
       1939   Slotki. Ed. by H. Freedman and M. Simon.
                   London: Soncino Press.

Origen   *Origène: Homélies sur les nombres*. Trans.
       1951   by A. Méhat. Paris: Editions du cerf.

Patte, D.   *What is Structural Exegesis?* Philadelphia:
       1976   Fortress Press.

Pettit, P.   *The Concept of Structuralism*. Berkeley:
       1975   University of California Press.

Piaget, J.   *Structuralism*. Trans. by C. Maschler.
       1970   New York: Harper & Row.

Polzin, R. M.   *Biblical Structuralism: Method and Sub-
       1977   jectivity in the Study of Ancient Texts*.
                   Philadelphia: Fortress Press.

Propp, V.   *Morphology of the Folktale*. Trans. by
       1968   L. Scott. 2nd ed. by L. A. Wagner. Austin:
                   University of Texas Press.

Rashi   *Pentateuch with Rashi's Commentary*. Trans.
       1933   by A. M. Silbermann, *et al*. London:
                   Shapiro, Vallentine & Co.

Ricoeur, P.   *The Conflict of Interpretations: Essays in
       1974   Hermeneutics*. Ed. by D. Ihde. Evanston:
                   Northwestern University Press.

Scholes, R. and   *The Nature of Narrative*. New York: Oxford
     R. Kellogg   University Press.
       1968

Smend, R.   "Das Wort Jahwes an Elia: Erwägungen zur Kom-
       1975   position von 1 Reg. xvii-xix". *VT* 25: 525-43.

98   The Sense of Biblical Narrative

Stoebe, H.-J.   "David und Mikal". Von Ugarit nach Qumran,
1961   ed. by J. Hempel and L. Rost. Berlin:
                     Alfred Töpelmann: 224-43.

1973   Das erste Buch Samuelis. Gütersloh: Gerd
                     Mohn.

Thompson, J. A.   "The Significance of the Verb Love in the
1974   David-Jonathan Narratives in I Samuel". VT
                     24: 334-38.

Tromp, N. M.   "Water and Fire on Mount Carmel: A Concil-
1975   iatory Suggestion". Bibl 56: 480-502.

Weiser, A.   The Old Testament: Its Formation and
1961   Development. Trans. by D. M. Barton. New
                     York: Association Press.

1966   "Die Legitimation des Königs David: Zur
                     Eigenart und Entstehung der sogenannten
                     Geschichte von Davids Aufstieg". VT 16:
                     325-54.

Weiss, M.   "Weiteres über die Bauformen des Erzählens
1965   in der Bibel". Bibl 46: 181-206.

Welsford, E.   The Fool: His Social and Literary History.
1935   New York: Farrar & Rinehart.

Willis, J. T.   "The Function of Comprehensive Anticipatory
1973   Redactional Joints in 1 Sam 16-18". ZAW
                     85: 294-314.

Würthwein, E.   "Die Erzählung vom Gottesurteil auf dem
1962   Karmel". ZTK 59: 131-44.

Indexes

A. Authors

Ackroyd, P.R.	5
Ap-Thomas, D.R.	88
Barthes, R.	10
Calloud, J.	1, 27, 29
Calvin, J.	34, 49, 61
Coats, G.W.	29, 44, 62
Conrad, J.	9, 20, 21, 25
Crespy, G.	27
Crites, S.	3
Crossan, J.D.	87
Culler, J.	28
Culley, R.C.	5, 37, 59, 61
De George, F.M.	4
De George, R.T.	4
De Vaux, R.	87
De Vries, S.J.	24
Delitzsch, F.	50, 53, 54, 56, 61
Detweiler, R.	89, 92
Eerdmans, B.D.	48
Gibson, A.B.	21
Ginzberg, L.	57, 58, 62
Gray, G.B.	45, 60
Gray, J.	87
Greimas, A.J.	1, 3, 15, 16, 26, 27, 33, 40, 42, 55, 61, 62, 66, 67, 70, 77, 89, 91
Gressmann, H.	48
Grønbaek, J.H.	9, 21, 22, 23, 24
Hertzberg, H.W.	5, 13, 20, 21, 25
Jacobson, R.	16
Jobling, D.	7, 8, 24, 87
Keil, C.F.	50, 53, 54, 56, 61
Kellogg. R.	4, 18, 19
Lane, M.	16, 17
Leach, E.	11, 16, 17, 21, 89, 92
Lévi-Strauss, C.	1, 2, 16, 17, 27, 28, 54, 57, 60, 89, 91
McCarthy, D.J.	5, 17, 24, 92
Malbon, E.S.	92
Montgomery, J.A.	83
Morgenstern, J.	9, 10, 20
Noth, M.	26, 48, 54, 61, 92
Origen	58
Patte, D.	1, 27, 66, 67, 90
Philo Judaeus	56, 58, 61
Piaget, J.	63
Polzin, R.M.	83, 89, 91, 92
Propp, V.	1, 9, 27, 65, 66, 67, 68, 69, 71, 73, 81, 82
Rashi	34
Scholes, R.	4, 18, 19
Smend, R.	64, 86, 87, 88
Stoebe, H.-J.	5, 10, 13, 14, 24, 25
Tromp, N.M.	64, 72, 84, 87, 88
Weiser, A.	6, 23
Weiss, M.	11
Welsford, E.	21
Willis, J.T.	25
Würthwein, E.	87, 88

B. Biblical References

This list omits references to 1 Sam 13-31in Chapter I, Num 11-12 in Chapter II, and 1 Kg 17-18 in Chapter III. An asterisk indicates several references to parts of a passage on the page(s) given.

Gen			Num		1 Sam		
1:28	58		2:2	50	10:7		10
3	48		10:29-32	60	11	62,	92
34:30	87		10:33-36	34	14:29		87
			11-12	91			
Ex			11:1	84	**2 Sam**		
			14:12	29			
2:21	49		14:28-35	49	3:14		9
3	49		20:1-13	54	7		6
4:6-7	33				11		24
7:1	49		**Deut**				
12:37-39	60, 61				**1 Kg**		
12:38	34, 41,		7:4	48			
	51, 57		8:4	62	16:15-		86
15:20	48		24:8-9	33	2 Kg 10:27		
15:22-17:7	59		28:59-61*	53	16:15-34		86
15:22-27*	59				16:16		85
16	59, 62		**Jos**		16:21	83,	85
16:15	53				16:26		63
17:1-7	54, 59		5:12	54	16:29-34	85,	86
17:5-6	59		6:18	87	19	85,	86
18*	59, 60		7:25	87		88	
18:2	49				19:2		86
24*	60		**Judg**		21:25		86
32	59						
32:10	29, 59		11:35	87	**1 Chr**		
32:32	59		19-21	62			
33:7	50				2:7		87
33:7-11	50, 51, 59		**1 Sam**				
33:11	49				**Prov**		
33:20-23	59		2:27-36	24			
36	50		4:8	53	2:16		48
			5:6	53			
Lev			7-15*	5			
			8-12	17			
13:4-6	33		9:1-10:16	10			
13:9-17*	33		9:16	8			

C.   Technical Terms

No attempt has been made to list all the uses of a term; the references listed will provide definition of the term, and sometimes illustration of its use. Where a term is used non-technically as well as technically (e.g. "narrative"), only the technical use is listed. Cognates may be regarded as included in each term (e.g. "redundant" in "redundancy"), unless there are separate entries for cognates.

Actant   15, 33, 66-67
Actantial   15, 33-34,
   (model, scheme)   35, 66,70,
                                        77, 78
Alimentary (code)   53-55
Binary   See "Opposition"
   opposition
CCP   34-35
Code   27, 28, 46-55
Combat (Propp)   65
Contract   66-67
Contradiction   16-17, 76
   (cf. "opposition")
Counter-counterprogram   34-35
Counterprogram   34-35
CP   34-35
Deceptive   42-44
   (veridiction)
Deep (structure)   17, 18, 55
Diachrony   17, 18
Domination   66-67
Epistemology   20-21, 42-46,
   (isotopy)   66-67, 78-79,
                                            91
Exchange of meaning 63-64, 81
False (veridiction)   42-44
Function (Propp)   65, 67
Geographical (code)   47, 83
Helper   15-16, 40,
                                 65-67, 86
Hero (Propp)   65
Hierarchical organization 41
   (isotopy)

Instigation   35, 40, 91
Isotopy   27-28, 40-46,
                                     49, 91
Iterative
Knowledge   See "epistemology"
Lack (Propp)   65, 67
Liquidation   See "lack"
Main program   34
Mediation   16-17, 23
MP   34
Myth   16-17, 56-57
Narrative   27, 28-40,
   (as opposed to   61, 82-83
   "semantic")
Onomastic (code)   48
Opposition   16-17, 49, 54
Paradigmatic   28-35, 61,
                          77-79, 90-91
Performance   66-67
Political (code)   47-49
Program   · 33-35,
                           70, 77-78
Qualification   65, 68
Quest   See "hero"
Redundancy   16-17, 18
Residue   28, 49
SA, SB, SC, SD   28
SDa, SDb   38
Secret (veridiction)   42-44
Semantic   27, 40-56,
                             61, 83-84
Sender (actant)   15

Story ("well-formed") 65-66, 67

Subject (actant)   15, 40, 44

Surface (structure)   17, 29-33

Synchrony   17, 18

Syntagm (Patte)   66-67

Syntagmatic   28-29, 36-39,
                      61, 79-80, 91-92

System   27, 50, 63-64

Temporal (code)   47

Topographical (code) 49-53

True (veridiction)   42-44

Veridiction   42-44
  (cf. epistemology)

Vertical (code)   51-52

Villain (Propp)   65

Volition   66-67